Fiona Goble's
FAIRY TALE KNITS

20 ENCHANTING CHARACTERS TO MAKE

Ivy Press

First published in the UK in 2012 by

Ivy Press

210 High Street
Lewes
East Sussex BN7 2NS
United Kingdom
www.ivypress.co.uk

British Library Cataloguing-in-Publication Data.
A catalogue record for this book is available
from the British Library

ISBN: 978-1-908005-46-5

This book was conceived,
designed and produced by
Ivy Press

Creative Director Peter Bridgewater
Publisher Sophie Collins
Editorial Director Tom Kitch
Senior Designer James Lawrence
Designer Andrew Milne
Photographer Andrew Perris
Illustrator Melvyn Evans

Printed in China

Colour origination by Ivy Press Reprographics

10 9 8 7 6 5 4 3 2 1

Important safety information
Many of the knitted figures are small or
have removable parts, making them a
choking hazard. They are not suitable
for children under the age of 36 months.

Contents

Introduction 4
Check Out Your Knitting Bag 6
Knitting Fundamentals 8
Fancy Stitches 11
Getting It Together 12
Finishing Touches 13

Little Red Riding Hood 14

How to Knit Little Red Riding Hood 18

How to Knit Grandmother 21

How to Knit the Wolf 24

Rapunzel 26

How to Knit Rapunzel 30

How to Knit Dame Gothel 32

How to Knit Rapunzel's Prince 35

Hansel & Gretel 38

How to Knit Hansel 42

How to Knit Gretel 45

How to Knit the Wicked Witch 47

Goldilocks & the Three Bears 50

How to Knit Goldilocks 54

How to Knit Mother Bear 56

How to Knit Father Bear 58

How to Knit Baby Bear 60

The Three Little Pigs 62

How to Knit the Three Little Pigs 66

Beauty & the Beast 68

How to Knit Beauty 72

How to Knit the Beast 74

How to Knit the Sisters 78

Index 80

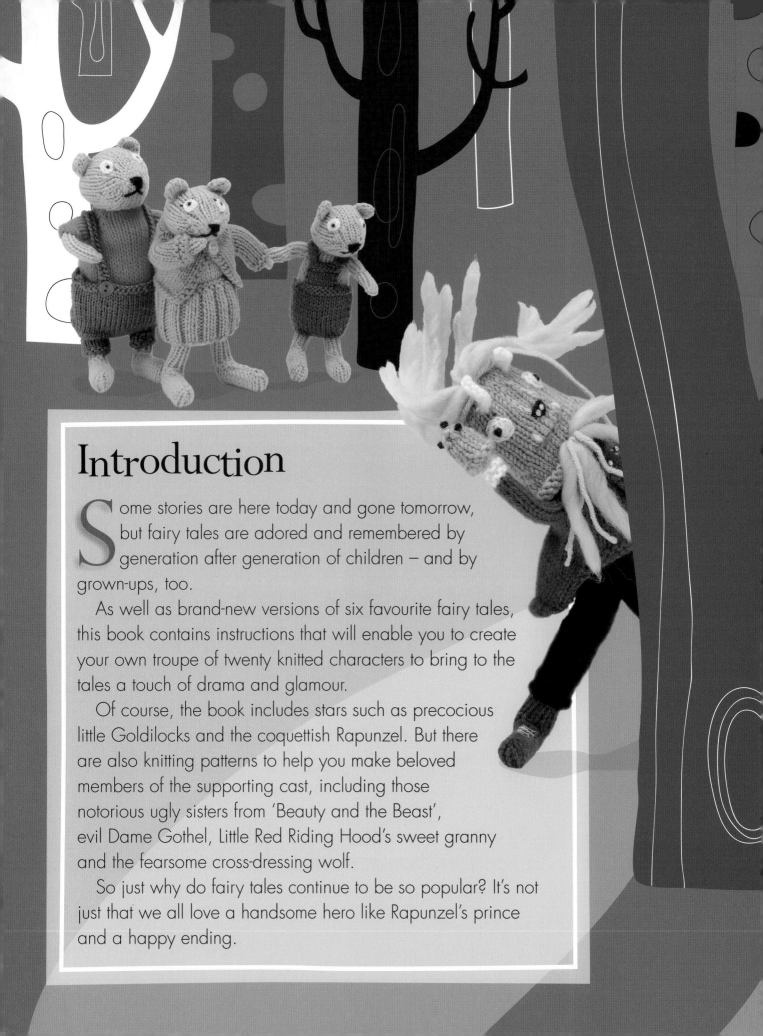

Introduction

Some stories are here today and gone tomorrow, but fairy tales are adored and remembered by generation after generation of children – and by grown-ups, too.

As well as brand-new versions of six favourite fairy tales, this book contains instructions that will enable you to create your own troupe of twenty knitted characters to bring to the tales a touch of drama and glamour.

Of course, the book includes stars such as precocious little Goldilocks and the coquettish Rapunzel. But there are also knitting patterns to help you make beloved members of the supporting cast, including those notorious ugly sisters from 'Beauty and the Beast', evil Dame Gothel, Little Red Riding Hood's sweet granny and the fearsome cross-dressing wolf.

So just why do fairy tales continue to be so popular? It's not just that we all love a handsome hero like Rapunzel's prince and a happy ending.

The stories in this book are packed with hardship, cruelty and danger lurking in familiar places, as the fairy-tale innocents Hansel, Gretel and Little Red Riding Hood discover. But, as the stories show, with some quick thinking and just a bit of good fortune, enemies such as the horrible hag in 'Hansel & Gretel', the devious wolf in 'Little Red Riding Hood' and the wicked witch who imprisoned poor, beautiful Rapunzel *can* be overcome.

Just in case you think modern living has become a bit superficial and sloppy, we're very pleased to include a tale that will help everyone understand that you really mustn't take what isn't yours, as the three woolly bears demonstrated to Goldilocks. And woe betide you if you don't act sensibly: a fate similar to that of two of the three little pink pigs may be yours . . . Finally, as Beauty eventually realizes when the beast removes his mask, if you judge a book entirely by its cover, you could be missing out on a real gem.

Check Out Your Knitting Bag

Even if you've only knitted a few projects before, you probably have most of what you need already in your knitting bag. However, to avoid the frustration of getting everything ready, only to realize something's missing, here is a list of all the essential items.

☑ Knitting Needles

You will need ordinary knitting needles (sometimes called single-pointed needles) in three sizes to make all the dolls in this book.

Because the dolls are small and you will not have many stitches on your needles at any one time, you will find shorter needles easier to work with. It is also a good idea to choose needles with quite pointed ends. The projects in this book are more tightly knitted than most garments and using pointed needles will make it easier to get the right tension.

A PAIR OF SIZE 2.75 MM (US 2)
You will need these to knit a few of the accessories – for example, the doll's shoes.

A PAIR OF SIZE 3 MM (US 2/3)
These are the basic needles that you will use to create the dolls and most of their outfits. If you think that you knit more tightly or more loosely than normal, you may need slightly bigger or smaller needles – so have a look at the guide to tension on page 7 to make sure.

A PAIR OF SIZE 3.75 MM (US 5)
You will need these to knit some of the characters' clothes.

☑ A Crochet Hook

You will need a size 3.25 mm (US D-3) or similar size crochet hook to make crochet chains for some of the dolls' clothes and hair.

☑ A Needle to Sew Your Work Together

You will need a needle with a fairly blunt end and an eye large enough for threading yarn to sew your dolls together. Sometimes, these are called 'yarn needles' – but a tapestry needle will do the job just as well.

☑ An Embroidery Needle

You will need an embroidery needle with an eye large enough for threading yarn to embroider your dolls' features. Embroidery needles are sharper than tapestry or yarn needles and having a sharp needle will make it much easier to work the necessary stitches.

☑ An Ordinary Sewing Needle

You will need this to sew the buttons, beads and sequins onto your dolls' clothes.

☑ A Stitch Holder, Large Safety Pin or Spare Knitting Needle

For some of the projects, you will need somewhere to hold spare stitches while you work on a different section of your knitting. You can choose a special knitting stitch holder or use a spare needle or large safety pin.

☑ A Measuring Tape or Ruler

You will need a measuring tape or ruler to measure lengths of yarn or the length of your crochet chains.

☑ A Pair of Small Scissors

These are essential for trimming the yarn tails after you have sewn your work together.

☑ Glue

You will probably find it easier to glue one or two of the trimmings in place, instead of sewing them on. Any PVA glue that dries clear is suitable for this.

☑ Red & Pink Colouring Pencils

The cheeks of the dolls are coloured by rubbing over the finished knitting with an ordinary colouring pencil. Don't be tempted to use a crayon or a felt-tipped pen, because the results will be disappointing.

A Water-Soluble Pen

This looks and works like an ordinary felt-tipped pen, but the ink disappears when it is sprayed or dabbed with water. Water-soluble pens are very useful for marking the position of your dolls' features before embroidering them. Before you use your pen, test it on the type of yarn you have used in the project, to make sure that the ink comes out easily.

A Row Counter

You can get several different types of row counters to help you keep track of how many rows you have worked. Some people find this useful, but it is not essential.

Yarns

All the dolls and their clothes in this book are knitted in double knitting (DK) yarn. DK yarn is available in 100 per cent wool, 100 per cent acrylic or a mix of wool and acrylic. It can also be made from cotton, silk or bamboo – or from these fibres mixed with wool and acrylic. It is recommended that you use either 100 per cent wool yarns or wool mixes (wool mixed with acrylic or other fibres). Cotton yarns and 100 per cent acrylic yarns can lead to disappointing results.

For some of the projects in this nook, you will also need small amounts of mohair yarn, bulky yarn and metallic crochet yarn.

Buttons, Beads, Bows & Sequins

Some of the dolls are adorned with a few small items such as buttons and beads. The ones recommended are a guide only; feel free to raid your sewing box to find inspiration for embellishing your creations.

Snap Fasteners

For a few of the projects, you will need some small snap fasteners. You can use either plastic or metal ones.

Polyester Toy Filling

The dolls are stuffed with a 100 per cent polyester toy filling that is specially made for stuffing hand-made items such as toys. Check that the filling you buy is safe and conforms to safety standards.

Sewing Thread

You will need some standard sewing thread to sew on items such as buttons, beads and sequins.

ABBREVIATIONS

The following abbreviations are used in the knitting patterns in this book.

*/**	these mark the start and end of a section of the knitting pattern to be repeated later when instructed	sl	slip one (slip a stitch onto the right-hand needle without knitting it)
( )	repeat the directions within the parentheses the number of times indicated	psso	pass slipped stitch over (pass the slipped stitch over the stitch just knitted)
[ ]	number in brackets refers to how many stitches you should have on your needle	ssk	slip, slip, knit (slip 2 stitches, one at a time, then knit the 2 slipped stitches together)
K	knit	rs	right side
P	purl	ws	wrong side
st(s)	stitch(es)	yf	yarn forward (bring the yarn from the back of the work to the front)
st st	stocking stitch		
beg	beginning		
cont	continue	rem	remaining
k2tog	knit the next 2 stitches together	rep	repeat
		g	gram
p2tog	purl the next 2 stitches together	oz	ounce
		mm	millimetre
kwise	by knitting the stitch	cm	centimetre
pwise	by purling the stitch	in	inch
inc1	increase one stitch (by knitting into the same stitch twice)	m	metre
		yd	yard
m1	make one stitch (by picking up the horizontal loop lying before the next stitch and knitting into the back of it)		

TENSION

The general knitting tension for the patterns in this book is 12 sts and 16 rows to 4 cm (1½-in) square over st st on 3 mm (US 2/3) needles.

With the dolls, tension is not as crucial as when knitting a garment. However, if your knitting is too loose, your dolls may end up looking rather shapeless and the stuffing may show through.

Knitting Fundamentals

Y ou do not need to know any complicated knitting techniques to knit the projects in this book. If you know how to knit and purl, to cast on and cast off and to increase and decrease, you will find all the items quite straightforward. If you need to brush up on any of these techniques, read on.

Casting On

You can cast on in several different ways but the recommended way, which gives your knitting a firm edge, is called cable casting on and uses two needles.

1 Make a slip knot by forming a loop in the yarn. With your knitting needle, pull a second loop of yarn through this loop. Then pull the knot up quite tightly. This slip knot forms the first cast-on stitch.

2 Hold the needle with the slip knot in your left hand. Pick up the other needle in your right hand and insert the point through the slip knot and under the left needle. Wind the yarn from your ball of wool (not the yarn 'tail') around the tip of the right needle.

3 Using the point of the right needle, draw the yarn through the slip knot to form a loop.

4 Transfer the loop, which is your new stitch, onto the left needle. You will now have two stitches on this needle.

5 To make the next stitch, insert the right needle between the two stitches on the left needle and wind the yarn over the right needle from left to right.

6 With the right needle, draw the yarn through the gap between the stitches to form a loop. Transfer the loop onto the left needle. There will now be three cast-on stitches on your needle.

Repeat the last two steps until you have the required number of stitches on your needle.

The Knit Stitch

This is the basic knitting stitch.

1 To make your first knit stitch, hold the needle with the cast-on stitches in your left hand and check that the working end of the yarn is at the back of the work. Insert the point of the right needle into the front of the first cast-on stitch, from left to right.

2 Wind the yarn round the point of the right needle, from left to right.

3 Using the tip of the right-hand needle, pull the yarn through the original stitch to form a loop on the right needle.

4 Slip the original stitch off the left needle by gently pulling the right-hand needle to the right. The new stitch is now on this needle.

Repeat the four steps above until you have knitted all the stitches on the left needle. To knit the next row, turn the work, transferring the needle from your right to your left hand.

The Purl Stitch

A purl stitch is rather like working a knit stitch backwards. Working alternate rows of knit and purl stitches creates a stitch known as stocking (stockinette) stitch, which is the main stitch used in this book. Purl stitches are generally worked with the reverse side of your work facing you, while knit stitches are worked on the right side of the work.

1 To make your first purl stitch, hold the needle with the stitches in your left hand and check that the working end of the yarn is at the front of the work. Insert the right needle through the front of the first stitch on the left needle, from right to left.

2 Wind the yarn around the needle from right to left.

3 With the tip of the right needle, pull the yarn through the original stitch to form a loop on the needle.

4 Slip the original stitch off the left needle by gently pulling the right-hand needle further to the right. The new stitch will now be on this needle.

Repeat the four steps above until you have purled all the stitches on the left needle. To purl the next row, turn the work, transferring the needle from your right to your left hand.

Casting Off

When you have finished your knitting, you will need to cast off to prevent your knitting from unravelling. Try not to cast off too tightly, as this can make it harder to sew your knitted pieces together.

CASTING OFF KNITWISE

The steps below describe how to cast off knitwise. This is the normal method of casting off on the right side of your work and also sometimes on the reverse of your work. If the pattern does not tell you to cast off in a specific way, you can assume that you need to cast off knitwise.

1 Knit two stitches in the normal way. Using the tip of the left needle, pick up the first stitch that you knitted and lift it over the second stitch.

2 You now have just one stitch on the right-hand needle; you can see that there is a neat loop across the top of the first cast-off stitch, so the yarn cannot unravel.

Knit another stitch, so that you have two stitches on the right-hand needle once more, and lift the first stitch over the second. Repeat this process until you have only one stitch left on the right needle. Trim the yarn, leaving a tail long enough to sew your knitting together. Pull the yarn tail all the way through the last stitch.

CASTING OFF PURLWISE

Sometimes you will need to cast off purlwise. Casting off purlwise is like casting off knitwise, except that you purl the stitches instead of knitting them.

1 Purl two stitches in the normal way. Using the point of the left needle, pick up the first stitch that you purled and lift it over the second stitch.

2 As with casting off knitwise, you now have just one stitch on the right-hand needle.

Purl another stitch, so that you have two stitches on the right-hand needle once more, and lift the first stitch over the second. Repeat this process until you have only one stitch left on the right needle. Trim the yarn, leaving a tail long enough to sew your knitting together. Pull the yarn tail all the way through the last stitch.

Increasing

Knitted pieces are shaped by increasing or decreasing the number of stitches on your needle as you knit. There are different ways of doing this and the method that you need will vary from project to project. The aim is to always make the increase as neat as possible.

INCREASING BY MAKING AN ADDITIONAL STITCH (M1)

1 At the point where you want the new stitch, pick up the horizontal strand that runs between the two stitches using the tip of your right-hand needle.

2 Transfer the strand to the left-hand needle by inserting the tip of the left-hand needle from right to left through the front of the strand.

3 Knit through the back of the new stitch and transfer the stitch to your right-hand needle.

INCREASING BY KNITTING INTO A STITCH TWICE (INC1)

Start by knitting the stitch in the normal way. However, instead of slipping the old stitch off the needle, knit through the back of it before sliding it off. The instruction 'inc1' refers to creating an additional stitch when you knit the next stitch.

Decreasing

DECREASING BY KNITTING TWO STITCHES TOGETHER (K2TOG)

To knit two stitches together, simply insert your needle through the front of two stitches instead of one, and then knit them in the normal way.

DECREASING BY PURLING TWO STITCHES TOGETHER (P2TOG)

To purl two stitches together, simply insert your needle through the front of two stitches instead of one, and then purl them in the normal way.

DECREASING BY SLIPPING 2 STITCHES, THEN KNITTING THEM TOGETHER (SSK)

Slip one stitch and then the next stitch onto your right-hand needle, without knitting them. Then insert the left-hand needle from left to right through the front loops of both slipped stitches and knit them in the normal way.

DECREASING TWO STITCHES AT A TIME (S1, K2TOG, PSSO)

1 Slip the first stitch from the left- to the right-hand needle without knitting it. Knit the next two stitches together.

2 Using the point of the left-hand needle, lift the slipped stitch over the stitch in front.

Sometimes, you will need to work this decrease on the wrong side of your work. In this case, simply slip the stitch purlwise, then purl the next two stitches together before passing the slipped stitch over.

Fancy Stitches

The main stitches that you will need for this book are garter stitch (where you knit every row), stocking stitch (alternate rows of knit and purl stitches) and ribbing (where you knit one stitch and purl the next). You will also need to know lace stitch and extended garter stitch.

Lace Stitch

This stitch creates a knitted row with a series of holes. It can be used to produce a lacy effect or folded across the holes to create a wavy or 'picot' edge. The holes can also be used for threading through a tie or cord.

On the right side of your work, bring the yarn to the front, under the right-hand needle.

Knit the next two stitches together, taking the yarn over the top of your needle to do this.

Extended Garter Stitch

For some items, you will need to work a special version of garter stitch.

1 Insert the right-hand needle into the stitch, as if you were knitting the stitch as normal. Instead of winding the yarn once around the needle, wind it around two or three times, as indicated in the pattern.

2 Continue knitting the stitch in the normal way, pulling all the loops through the stitch.

The row after the 'extended' row is knitted in the normal way, dropping the extra loops as you go to create the extended stitch.

Crocheting a Chain

The projects do not involve much crochet as such, but you will need to know how to make a simple crochet chain for some of the dolls and clothes.

1 Make a slip knot on the crochet hook, as if you were starting to cast on some knitting. Holding the slip stitch on the hook, wind the yarn around the hook from the back to the front. Then catch the yarn in the crochet hook tip.

2 Pull the yarn through the slip stitch on your crochet hook to make the second link in the chain.

Continue in this way until the chain is the length that you need.

Reshaping

Sometimes, the small garments that you create for your characters do not look exactly right. There is nothing wrong with your knitting – it is just that the items are small and yarns behave in certain ways. If you are not happy with the shape of a garment, simply soak the item in lukewarm water and squeeze it gently. Shape it while it is wet and leave it to dry.

Getting It Together

Piecing your work together is one of the best things about knitting the dolls in this book, because it's at this moment that you can really see your characters taking shape. Always join your pieces using the same yarn that you used to knit your item, changing colours along the same seam, if necessary. Take your time, particularly at first, to make sure that your work is neat and even.

Mattress Stitch

You can use one version of this stitch to join vertical seams and a different version to join horizontal edges. This joining technique produces a seam that is almost invisible.

VERTICAL EDGES

To join two vertical edges with mattress stitch, place the two pieces of knitting side by side. Take the needle under the running stitch between the first two stitches on one side, and then under the corresponding running stitch between the first two stitches on the other side. Continue in this way, pulling the yarn up fairly tightly every few stitches.

HORIZONTAL EDGES

To join two horizontal edges, take the needle under the two 'legs' of the last row of stitches on one piece of knitting, then under the two 'legs' of the corresponding stitch on the other piece of knitting. Continue in this way, pulling the yarn up fairly tightly every few stitches.

You can use a variation of mattress stitch to join small pieces such as the limbs to the main body.

Oversewing

This is the best way to join together two small pieces at a seam or to join pieces with curved edges. It is normally worked with the right sides of the two pieces together.

The stitch is worked by taking the needle from the front of your work, over the edge of the seam and out through the front again.

A version of oversewing is also used to join very small pieces of knitting, such as the ears and shoes, to the main part of the doll.

Picking Up Stitches Along an Edge

Occasionally, you will need to pick up stitches along an edge and knit onto these stitches.

With the right side of the work facing you, insert the needle into the stitch where you need to begin picking up and knit into it the normal way.

Finishing Touches

Finishing your work in a tidy and orderly way and adding just the right final touches can make all the difference to the look of your knitted items. So don't rush – and take extra care to get just the look that you want.

Concealing & Weaving in Ends

When you have finished knitting your items and sewing them together, there will probably be some yarn tails that need concealing.

On the dolls themselves, you can simply take your needle into the body and outside at another point. Pull the yarn and squash the body slightly, then trim the yarn close to the surface. When the body springs back into shape, the yarn tail will disappear into the middle of the doll and be invisible.

After knitting the dolls' clothes, the easiest way to weave in the ends is to work a few small running stitches forwards and then backwards in the garment's seam. Then trim the yarn very close to the surface. You might want to use an embroidery needle for this and work between the threads, because this will help the yarn stay in place.

Embroidery

There are a few basic embroidery stitches you will need to know in order to create your characters' features.

STARTING & FINISHING

When you start your embroidery, tie a simple knot at the end of your yarn. Take the needle into the back of your work, between stitches, in an inconspicuous area, then bring it out again at your starting point. Pull gently but firmly on the yarn, so that the knot slips through the stitches and embeds itself somewhere in the middle of your doll.

When you have finished your embroidery, take your yarn out to an inconspicuous area and work a couple of very small stitches, one on top of the other, in the running stitches between the knitted stitches (these will be slightly sunken). Then conceal the yarn end using the method described above.

STRAIGHT STITCH

This stitch is used for some of the characters' mouths and eyelashes. It is one of the easiest stitches and simply involves bringing the thread out at one point and taking it down again at another point.

CHAIN STITCH

This embroidery stitch is used for the whites of the eyes, some of the noses and some of the hair.

Bring the needle out at the point where you want the stitch to start. Then take the needle back into the knitting, just next to the starting point, to create a little loop of yarn. Bring the needle back up through the knitting a stitch width along and catch in the loop. Pull your thread up gently until the stitch is quite firm.

FRENCH KNOT

This stitch is used for the pupils of the eyes and for the nostrils.

Bring the yarn out at the point where you want to work the knot. With the needle close to the surface of the knitting, wind the yarn twice around the needle. Then take the tip of the needle back into the knitting, just to the side of your starting point. Continue pulling the needle through your work and slide the knot off the needle and onto your knitting.

SATIN STITCH

This stitch is used for some of the characters' noses and is really a series of straight stitches worked very closely together.

Bring the needle out at the point where you want to start. Insert the needle back into the work and bring it out again near the starting point, ready to work the next stitch. Continue in this way until the shape is filled. To neaten your satin stitch, you can work a single straight stitch down the sides to conceal the beginning and ends of the stitches.

Little Red Riding Hood

One day, Red Riding Hood's mother said to her, **"Now, Granny's not been well – take this** basket of treats to her and be back as quick as you can!" Red Riding Hood set off through the forest. She wasn't certain of the path, so she was relieved to meet a handsome stranger in a sleek fur coat. **"Please sir, I'm not too sure where my granny's cottage is . . ." "Oh yes,"** said the Wolf, **"Go this way, little girl – it won't take long!"** As soon as she'd turned the corner, Wolfie bounded round to Grandma's using a short cut. He'd hatched a plan to eat the old lady and the little girl – and finish off with the basket of fruit and cakes. Yum yum! Leaping through the door, he gobbled up the old lady in a couple of gulps, slipped into her clothes (they were a bit tight) and scrambled into bed, pulling the covers up high.

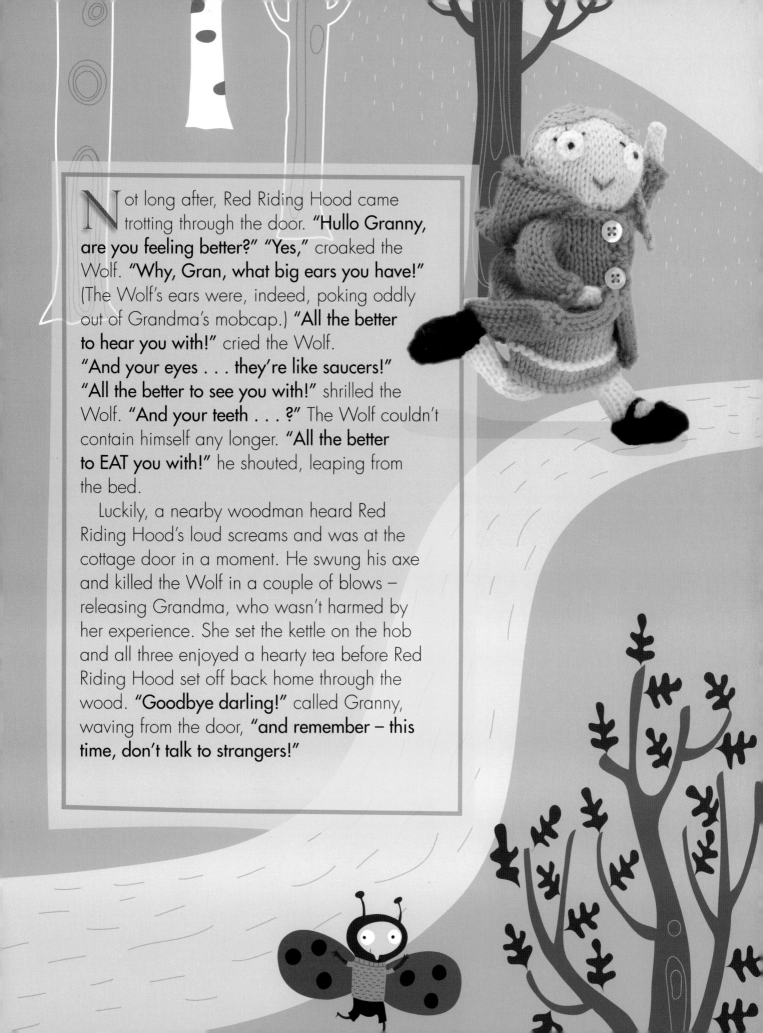

Not long after, Red Riding Hood came trotting through the door. "Hullo Granny, are you feeling better?" "Yes," croaked the Wolf. "Why, Gran, what big ears you have!" (The Wolf's ears were, indeed, poking oddly out of Grandma's mobcap.) "All the better to hear you with!" cried the Wolf. "And your eyes . . . they're like saucers!" "All the better to see you with!" shrilled the Wolf. "And your teeth . . . ?" The Wolf couldn't contain himself any longer. "All the better to EAT you with!" he shouted, leaping from the bed.

Luckily, a nearby woodman heard Red Riding Hood's loud screams and was at the cottage door in a moment. He swung his axe and killed the Wolf in a couple of blows – releasing Grandma, who wasn't harmed by her experience. She set the kettle on the hob and all three enjoyed a hearty tea before Red Riding Hood set off back home through the wood. "Goodbye darling!" called Granny, waving from the door, "and remember – this time, don't talk to strangers!"

Little Red Riding Hood

She's wrapped up tightly in her brand new, woolly coat, knitted in a dashing scarlet yarn. Now Little Red Riding Hood is ready for the trek through the forest to take the basket of food to her ailing grandmother.

YOU WILL NEED

2 g/¹⁄₁₆ oz (4 m/4½ yd) pale pink DK yarn

3.5 g/⅛ oz (8 m/9 yd) green DK yarn

6 g/¼ oz (14 m/15½ yd) flesh DK yarn

1 g/¹⁄₁₆ oz (2.5 m/3 yd) ochre DK yarn

3.5 g/⅛ oz (8.5 m/9½ yd) white DK yarn

7.5 g/¼ oz (18 m/20 yd) pale blue DK yarn

14.5 g/½ oz (34 m/37 yd) bright red DK yarn

2 g/¹⁄₁₆ oz (5 m/5½ yd) black DK yarn

Very small amount of mauve DK yarn

2 small white buttons

2 small snap fasteners

Red sewing thread

10–15 g/⅜–½ oz polyester toy filling

Red colouring pencil

Use size 3 mm (US 2/3) knitting needles, except when instructed to use size 2.75 mm (US 2) knitting needles.

DOLL

BODY & HEAD

The body and head are knitted together from the base of the body upwards and include the underpants and top.

Front

Make 1

❋ Cast on 13 sts in pale pink.
❋ Work 7 rows in st st, beg with a K row.
❋ Next row: K.
❋ Break pale pink yarn and join green yarn.
❋ Work 11 rows in st st, beg with a K row.
❋ Next row: K.
❋ Break green yarn and join flesh yarn.
❋ Next row: K.
❋ Next row: (p2tog) twice, P to last 4 sts, (p2tog) twice. [9 sts]
❋ Next row: K1, inc1 into next 6 sts, K2. [15 sts]
❋ Next row: P.
❋ Next row: K1, inc1, K to last 3 sts, inc1, K2. [17 sts]
❋ Next row: P.*
❋ Rep last 2 rows twice more. [21 sts]
❋ Work 2 rows in st st, beg with a K row.
❋ Next row: K2, (k2tog) twice, K9, (ssk) twice, K2. [17 sts]
❋ Next row: p2tog, P to last 2 sts, p2tog. [15 sts]
❋ Next row: K2, (k2tog) twice, K3, (ssk) twice, K2. [11 sts]
❋ Next row: p2tog, P to last 2 sts, p2tog. [9 sts]
❋ Cast off.

Back

Make 1

❋ Work as for front to *.
❋ Break flesh yarn and join ochre yarn.
❋ Next row: K1, inc1, K to last 3 sts, inc1, K1. [19 sts]
❋ Next row: P.
❋ Rep last 2 rows once more. [21 sts]
❋ Work 2 rows in st st, beg with a K row.
❋ Next row: K2, (k2tog) twice, K9, (ssk) twice, K2. [17 sts]
❋ Next row: p2tog, P to last 2 sts, p2tog. [15 sts]

❋ Next row: K2, (k2tog) twice, K3, (ssk) twice, K2. [11 sts]
❋ Next row: p2tog, P to last 2 sts, p2tog. [9 sts]
❋ Cast off.

LEGS

The socks and legs are knitted as one piece, starting at the sole of the foot.

Make 2

❋ Cast on 20 sts in white.
❋ Work 4 rows in st st, beg with a K row.
❋ Next row: K5, cast off 10 sts, K5. [10 sts]
❋ Work 4 rows in st st, beg with a P row.
❋ Next row: K.
❋ Break white yarn and join flesh yarn.
❋ Work 10 rows in st st, beg with a K row.
❋ Cast off.

ARMS

The arms are knitted from the top of the shoulder to the tip of the hand.

Make 2

❋ Cast on 7 sts in green.
❋ Work 7 rows in st st, beg with a K row.
❋ Next row: K.
❋ Next row: P.
❋ Break green yarn and join flesh yarn.
❋ Work 11 rows in st st, beg with a P row.
❋ Next row: K1, k2tog, K1, ssk, K1. [5 sts]
❋ Next row: p2tog, P1, p2tog. [3 sts]
❋ Next row: s1, k2tog, psso. [1 st]
❋ Break yarn and pull it through rem st.

MAKING UP

With the front and back body and head pieces right sides together, oversew around the head. Turn the piece right side out and sew the side seams of the body using mattress stitch, leaving the lower edge open for stuffing. Stuff the doll and close the gap, using mattress stitch.

Fold one leg in half lengthways, right sides together, and oversew the top and lower edge of the foot. Turn the leg right side out and sew the long seam, using mattress stitch. Repeat with the second leg. Stuff the legs and feet.

Fold one arm in half lengthways, right sides together, and oversew around the hand. Turn the arm right side out and sew the long seam, using mattress stitch. Repeat with the second arm. The arms do not need stuffing.

Sew the arms and legs in place.

Using ochre yarn, work a few rows of chain stitch at the front of the head for the hair. For the plaits, cut a 40-cm (16-in) length of ochre yarn. Hold the two yarn ends in one hand and insert your finger of the other hand in the loop. Holding the yarn taught, wind your finger to produce the cord. It will twist back on itself to produce a 4-strand cord. The twisted cords should be about 4 cm (1.5 in) long. Work the second plait in the same way. Use the ends of the cord to fasten the plaits to the sides of the head.

Work two French knots in black yarn for the eyes. Work two circles of chain stitch around each eye, using white yarn. Using a separated strand of black yarn, work three straight stitches above each eye to represent the eyelashes.

Work a small V-shaped mouth in straight stitches, using mauve yarn. Colour the cheeks using a red colouring pencil.

SKIRT

Make 1

❋ Cast on 38 sts in pale blue.
❋ Work 3 rows in st st, beg with a P row.
❋ Leave pale blue yarn at side and join white yarn.
❋ K 2 rows. Break white yarn and use pale blue yarn.
❋ Work 8 rows in st st, beg with a K row.
❋ Next row: (k2tog) 9 times, K2, (ssk) 9 times. [20 sts]
❋ K 2 rows.
❋ Cast off.

MAKING UP

Sew the back seam of the skirt, using mattress stitch.

CLOAK

The main part of the cloak is knitted as one piece. The sleeves and hood are sewn on separately.

Make 1

❋ Cast on 28 sts in bright red.

❋ K 2 rows.

❋ Next row: K2, P6. Turn work and cont on these 8 sts only, leaving rem sts on needle.

❋ Next row: K.

❋ Next row: K2, P6.

❋ Rep these 2 rows once more.

❋ Break yarn and join it to rem sts on ws of work.

❋ Next row: P12. Turn work and cont on these 12 sts only, leaving rem sts on needle.

❋ Work 4 rows in st st, beg with a K row.

❋ Break yarn and join it to rem 8 sts on ws of work.

❋ Next row: P6, K2.

❋ Next row: K.

❋ Rep last 2 rows once more.

❋ Next row: P6, K2.

❋ Now work across all 28 sts.

❋ Next row: K6, m1, K4, m1, K8, m1, K4, m1, K6. [32 sts]

❋ Next row: K2, P to last 2 sts, K2.

❋ Next row: K.

❋ Next row: K2, P to last 2 sts, K2.

❋ Next row: K7, m1, K4, m1, K10, m1, K4, m1, K7. [36 sts]

❋ Next row: K.

❋ Next row: (K2, m1) to last 2 sts, K2. [53 sts]

❋ Next row: K2, P to last 2 sts, K2.

❋ Next row: K.

❋ Rep these 2 rows 6 times more.

❋ K 2 rows.

❋ Cast off.

SLEEVES

Make 2

❋ Cast on 12 sts in bright red.

❋ Work 13 rows in st st, beg with a K row.

❋ K 2 rows.

❋ Cast off.

HOOD

The hood is knitted from the face edge to the back.

Make 1

❋ Cast on 26 sts in bright red.

❋ K 2 rows.

❋ Work 15 rows in st st, beg with a P row.

❋ Cast off.

MAKING UP

Sew the seams of the sleeves, using mattress stitch. Insert them into the armholes of the coat and oversew them in place from the inside.

Fold the hood piece in half widthways and sew the back seam. Oversew the hood in place around the neck edge of the coat. The edges of the hood should come just to the front of the armhole edges.

Sew the buttons onto the right side of the coat. Sew the tops of the snap fasteners under the buttons and the bottoms of the snap fasteners to the corresponding part of the other side of the coat.

SHOES

Make 2

❋ Using size 2.75 mm (US 2) needles, cast on 8 sts in black.

❋ 1st row: inc1, K to last 2 sts, inc1, K1. [10 sts]

❋ Next row: P.

❋ Rep last 2 rows once more. [12 sts]

❋ Next row: inc1, K to last 2 sts, inc1, K1. [14 sts]

❋ Next row: P5, cast off 4 sts pwise, P to end. Turn work and cont on these last 5 sts only, leaving rem sts on needle or on a safety pin.

❋ Work 6 rows in st st, beg with a K row.

❋ Cast off.

❋ With rs facing, rejoin yarn to rem sts.

❋ Work 6 rows in st st, beg with a K row.

❋ Cast off.

MAKING UP

Fold the shoe pieces in half lengthways with the right side facing inwards. Oversew the back and lower seam of the shoes. Turn the right way out, put the shoes on the doll and secure with a couple of stitches. Then work a couple of large straight stitches across the foot to represent the bar of the shoe.

HOW TO KNIT
The Grandmother

She might be knocking on in years and not feeling too great at the moment, but most of the time Granny enjoys her life in her little cottage in the wood. So often Granny plays second fiddle to her famous granddaughter, but now you can help her shine by knitting your very own sweet little old lady in shades of yarn suited to her age.

DOLL

HEAD
The head is knitted from the base of the chin to the top of the forehead.
Make 2 pieces
❉ Cast on 6 sts in flesh.
❉ 1st row: K1, inc1, K2, inc1, K1. [8 sts]
❉ Next row: P.
❉ Next row: K1, m1, K to last st, m1, K1.
 [10 sts]
❉ Next row: P.
❉ Rep last 2 rows twice more. [14 sts]
❉ Work 10 rows in st st, beg with a K row.
❉ Next row: K2, k2tog, K6, ssk, K2. [12 sts]
❉ Next row: p2tog, P to last 2 sts, p2tog.
 [10 sts]
❉ Cast off.

BODY
The body is knitted from the lower edge to the neck edge and includes the corset.
Make 2 pieces
❉ Cast on 12 sts in pale pink.
❉ Work 8 rows in st st, beg with a K row.
❉ Next row: K2, k2tog, K4, ssk, K2. [10 sts]
❉ Next row: K.

❋ Work 6 rows in st st, beg with a K row.

❋ Next row: K2, m1, K6, m1, K2. [12 sts]

❋ Work 3 rows in st st, beg with a P row.

❋ Break pale pink yarn and join flesh yarn.

❋ Work 2 rows in st st, beg with a K row.

❋ Next row: Cast off 1 st, K to end. [11 sts]

❋ Next row: Cast off 1 st pwise, P to end. [10 sts]

❋ Cast off.

LEGS

The feet and legs are knitted as one piece, starting at the sole of the foot.
Make 2

❋ Cast on 24 sts in flesh.

❋ Work 4 rows in st st, beg with a K row.

❋ Next row: K5, cast off 14 sts, K to end. [10 sts]

❋ Work 21 rows in st st, beg with a P row.

❋ Cast off.

ARMS

The arms are knitted from the top of the shoulder to the tip of the hand.
Make 2

❋ Cast on 9 sts in flesh.

❋ Work 18 rows in st st, beg with a K row.

❋ Next row: K2, k2tog, K1, ssk, K2. [7 sts]

❋ Next row: p2tog, P3, p2tog. [5 sts]

❋ Next row: k2tog, K1, ssk. [3 sts]

❋ Break yarn and thread through rem sts.

HAIR

❋ Work five 16-cm (6½-in) crochet chains in pale grey.

MAKING UP

Place the two head pieces right sides together and oversew around the edges, leaving the top of the head open for turning and stuffing. Turn the head right side out, stuff and close the gap, using mattress stitch. Sew the body together using mattress stitch, leaving the lower edge open for turning and stuffing. Stuff and close the gap. Sew the head to the body.

Fold one leg in half lengthways, right sides together, and oversew the top and lower edge of the foot. Turn the leg right side out and sew the back seam, using mattress stitch. Repeat with the second leg. Stuff the legs and feet.

Fold one arm in half lengthways, right sides together, and oversew around the hand. Turn the hand right side out and sew the long seam, using mattress stitch. Repeat with the second arm. The arms do not need stuffing.

Sew the arms and legs in place.

Arrange the crochet chains for the hair on the head and stitch in place.

Work two French knots in black yarn for the eyes. Work a circle of chain stitch around each eye, using white yarn. Using flesh yarn, work a flattened coil of chain stitches for the nose and a straight stitch above each eye to represent the eyelids.

Using deep pink yarn, work two straight stitches side by side for the mouth, so that they form a flattened V shape. Colour the cheeks and across the nose using the red colouring pencil.

NIGHTDRESS

Make 2 pieces

❋ Cast on 18 sts in pale turquoise.

❋ 1st row: K1, (yf, k2tog) to last st, K1. [18 sts]

❋ Next row: P.

❋ Rep last 2 rows once more.

❋ Next row: K1, (yf, k2tog) to last st, K1. [18 sts]

❋ Next row: K.

❋ Work 20 rows in st st, beg with a K row.

❋ Next row: k2tog, (yf, k2tog) to last 2 sts, ssk. [16 sts]

❋ Next row: p2tog, P to last 2 sts, p2tog. [14 sts]

❋ Next row: K2, k2tog, K to last 4 sts, ssk, K2. [12 sts]

❋ Work 7 rows in st st, beg with a P row.

❋ K 2 rows.

❋ Cast off pwise.

TIE

Make 1

❋ Using pale pink yarn, work a 21-cm (8½-in) crochet chain. Trim and fray the ends.

MAKING UP

Oversew 5 mm (³⁄₁₆ in) at each side of the cast-off edge to form the neck hole. Join the side seams using mattress stitch, leaving the top 2.5 cm (1 in) open to form the armholes. Thread the tie through the eyelets at the waist and fasten in a knot at the side.

SLIPPERS

Make 2

❋ Using size 2.75 mm (US 2) needles, cast on 8 sts in pale pink.

❋ 1st row: inc1, K to last 2 sts, inc1, K1. [10 sts]

❋ Next row: P.

❋ Rep last 2 rows once more. [12 sts]

❋ Work 2 rows in st st, beg with a K row.

❋ Next row: inc1, K to last 2 sts, inc1, K1. [14 sts]

❋ Next row: P5, cast off 4 sts pwise, P to end. Turn work and cont on these last 5 sts only, leaving rem sts on needle or on a safety pin.

❋ Work 6 rows in st st, beg with a K row.

❋ Cast off.

❋ With rs facing, rejoin yarn to rem sts.

❋ Work 6 rows in st st, beg with a K row.

❋ Cast off.

BOWS

Make 2

❋ Work a 6-cm (2½-in) crochet chain in white.

MAKING UP

Fold the slipper pieces in half lengthways with the right side facing inward. Oversew the back and lower seams. Turn the right way out. Put the slippers on the doll and secure with a couple of stitches. Arrange the bows in figure-of-eight shapes with the yarn tails at the centre, and use these tails to stitch the bows in place.

BED JACKET

The main part of the bed jacket is knitted as one piece from the neck edge downwards.
Make 1

❋ Cast on 26 sts in pale yellow.

❋ K 2 rows.

* Next row: K2, P4. Turn and work on these 6 sts only, leaving rem sts on needle.
* Next row: K.
* Next row: K2, P4.
* Rep these last 2 rows once more. Break yarn and join it to rem sts on ws of work.
* Next row: P14. Turn and work on these 14 sts only, leaving rem sts on needle.
* Work 4 rows in st st, beg with a K row. Break yarn and join it to rem 6 sts on ws of work.
* Next row: P4, K2.
* Next row: K.
* Rep last 2 rows once more.
* Next row: P4, K2.
* Next row: K across all 26 sts.
* Next row: K2, P to last 2 sts, K2.
* Next row: K8, m1, K10, m1, K8. [28 sts]
* Next row: K2, P to last 2 sts, K2.
* Next row: K8, m1, K12, m1, K8. [30 sts]
* Next row: K2, (yf, k2tog) to last 2 sts, K2. [30 sts]
* K 2 rows.
* Cast off loosely.

SLEEVES

The sleeves are knitted from the armhole edge to the cuff.
Make 2
* Cast on 12 sts in pale yellow.
* Work 11 rows in st st, beg with a K row.

* K 2 rows.
* Cast off.

MAKING UP

Sew the sleeve seems using mattress stitch and oversew the sleeves in place around the armholes from the inside of the jacket.

BLOOMERS

The bloomers are knitted as one piece.
Make 1
* Cast on 16 sts in pale pink for first leg.
* K 2 rows.
* Work 3 rows in st st, beg with a P row.
* Break yarn and leave sts on a stitch holder or spare needle.
* Work second leg in the same way, but do not break yarn.
* Next row: K 16 sts from leg just knitted then 16 sts from first leg. [32 sts]
* Next row: P.
* Next row: K8, m1, K16, m1, K8. [34 sts]
* Next row: P.
* Next row: K8, m1, K1, m1, K16, m1, K1, m1, K8. [38 sts]
* Work 7 rows in st st, beg with a P row.
* Next row: K2, (yf, k2tog) to last 2 sts, K2. [38 sts]
* K 2 rows.
* Cast off loosely.

MAKING UP

Fold the two sides inwards to create the basic bloomer shape. Sew the inside leg seams and the back seam, using mattress stitch. For the cord, work a 20-cm (8-in) crochet chain in white. Thread the cord through the eyelets at the waist edge.

HAT

Make 2 pieces
* Cast on 18 sts in white.
* Work 3 rows in st st, beg with a P row.
* Next row: K1, (yf, k2tog) to last st, K1. [18 sts]
* K 2 rows.
* Next row: P.
* Next row: K.
* Next row: p2tog, P to last 2 sts, p2tog. [16 sts]
* Next row: K1, (k2tog) twice, K to last 5 sts, (ssk) twice, K1. [12 sts]
* Next row: p2tog, P to last 2 sts, p2tog. [10 sts]
* Cast off.

MAKING UP

With the hat pieces right sides together, oversew around the sides and top. Work an 8-cm (3¼-in) crochet chain in pale turquoise yarn, tie it in a bow and fasten it to the front of the hat.

HOW TO KNIT
The Wolf

He may be knitted in a gorgeous soft grey yarn, but this wolf is one tricky and deceitful creature. With his sly smile, he's all friendly and sweet-talking one minute. The next minute he's baring his teeth and hell bent on grabbing himself a decent meal. Use him again in the story of the Three Little Pigs.

YOU WILL NEED

20 g/¾ oz (50 m/55 yd) grey DK yarn
Small amounts of black, white and mid-pink DK yarns
10–15 g/⅜–½ oz polyester toy filling

Use size 3 mm (US 2/3) knitting needles, except when instructed to use size 2.75 mm (US 2) knitting needles.

DOLL

HEAD

The head is knitted from the back to the front.

Make 2 pieces

⁂ Cast on 15 sts in grey.
⁂ Work 8 rows in st st, beg with a K row.
⁂ Next row: K2, m1, K11, m1, K2. [17 sts]
⁂ Work 3 rows in st st, beg with a P row.
⁂ Next row; K2, k2tog, K to last 4 sts, ssk, K2. [15 sts]
⁂ Next row: P.
⁂ Rep last 2 rows 4 times more. [7 sts]
⁂ Next row: K1, k2tog, K1, ssk, K1. [5 sts]
⁂ Next row: P.
⁂ Next row: k2tog, K1, ssk. [3 sts]
⁂ Next row: s1, p2tog, psso. [1 st]
⁂ Break yarn and pull it through rem st.

EARS

Make 2

⁂ Using size 2.75 mm (US 2) needles, cast on 6 sts in grey.
⁂ K 6 rows.
⁂ Next row: k2tog, K2, ssk. [4 sts]
⁂ K 2 rows.
⁂ Next row: k2tog, ssk. [2 sts]
⁂ Next row: k2tog. Break yarn and pull it through rem st.

BODY

The body is knitted from the bottom edge upwards.

Make 2 pieces

⁂ Cast on 14 sts in grey.
⁂ Work 6 rows in st st, beg with a K row.
⁂ Next row: K2, m1, K to last 2 sts, m1, K2. [16 sts]
⁂ Next row: P.
⁂ Rep last 2 rows 3 times more. [22 sts]

⁂ Work 10 rows in st st, beg with a P row.
⁂ Next row: K2, k2tog, K to last 4 sts, ssk, K2. [20 sts]
⁂ Work 3 rows in st st, beg with a P row.
⁂ Next row: K2, k2tog, K to last 4 sts, ssk, K2. [18 sts]
⁂ Next row: P.
⁂ Rep last 2 rows 4 more times. [10 sts]
⁂ Work 4 rows in st st, beg with a K row.
⁂ Cast off.

LEGS

The feet and legs are knitted in one piece, starting at the sole of the foot.

Make 2

⁂ Cast on 30 sts in grey.
⁂ Work 4 rows in st st, beg with a K row.
⁂ Next row: K4, cast off 22 sts, K4. [8 sts]
⁂ Work 9 rows in st st, beg with a P row.
⁂ Cast off.

ARMS

The arms are knitted from the top edge to the paw.

Make 2

⁂ Cast on 8 sts in grey.
⁂ Work 16 rows in st st, beg with a K row.
⁂ Next row: K1, k2tog, K2, ssk, K1. [6 sts]
⁂ Next row: p2tog, P2, p2tog. [4 sts]
⁂ Cast off.

MAKING UP

With the two head pieces wrong sides together, sew the sides using mattress stitch, leaving the back edge open for stuffing. Stuff the head and close the gap using mattress stitch. With the two body pieces wrong sides together, sew the sides and lower edge using mattress stitch. Stuff the body through the neck edge. Position the head on the neck so that the neck forms a circle on the underside of the head and stitch it in place.

Fold one leg in half in half lengthways, right sides together, and oversew the top and bottom of the foot. Turn the leg right side out and sew the back seam using mattress stitch. Repeat with the second leg. Stuff and sew in place.

Fold one arm in half lengthways, right sides together, and oversew around the paw. Turn the arm right side out and sew the long seam using mattress stitch. Repeat with the second arm. The arms do not need stuffing. Sew the arms in place.

Sew the ears in place, curving them slightly at the base.

Work two French knots in black yarn for the eyes. Work two circles of chain stitch around each eye, using white yarn. Work a small coil of chain stitch in black yarn for the nose. Work a row of chain stitch in mid-pink yarn for the mouth and work a row of running stitch over the chain stitch in white yarn for the teeth.

Rapunzel

When Rapunzel was just a tiny baby, her father offended Dame Gothel, a powerful witch. As a punishment, the Dame forced him to give her his baby daughter. She kept the little girl under lock and key: Rapunzel saw nothing of the outside world, nor did she meet anyone but the witch. As she got older, she grew beautiful and accomplished, with golden hair that was startlingly long and shiny. In her own wicked way, Dame Gothel loved the girl and was always afraid that her prize might escape, so she locked Rapunzel up in a tall tower that didn't even have a staircase or a door.

As before, Rapunzel saw no one but the Dame: when Gothel arrived at the tower, she would call up to its window, saying, **"Rapunzel, Rapunzel, let down your hair!"** and the girl would hang her heavy golden plait out of the window for the witch to clamber up. Hand over hand, Gothel would laboriously climb up Rapunzel's hair, hauling with her a basket of food, and the other things – books and sewing materials – with which she expected the girl to fill the long hours until her next visit.

The tower looked out onto a lonely landscape and few people passed by. One day, however, a prince came down the deserted road (he'd been out hunting and had lost his way). The tower intrigued him, and, as he approached, he heard a girl's voice, singing sweetly, coming through the window. Walking around the tower's base he could not find a door, so he called up to the window. **"I say, who's singing? Do you live there? Lean out so that I can see your face!"** So Rapunzel leant from the window and, for the first time, saw a man (and a handsome one, at that).

Rapunzel was immediately intrigued; when the prince asked how he could talk to her, she let down her hair and told him to climb up it, and he eagerly did so. The prince was entranced by Rapunzel's wit and beauty, but he couldn't understand why she was in such a deserted place and all alone. For a week, he visited every afternoon (Gothel came in the mornings, so by chance they never met). But on the eighth day, Rapunzel carelessly said to Gothel, as she clambered up her hair, **"You know, it's funny – you're much heavier than the prince."** And so the truth came out. Gothel flew into a rage, cut off the girl's beautiful hair and threw Rapunzel from the tower. Bruised and shocked, she wandered away into the wilderness.

That afternoon, when the prince came and called for Rapunzel, Gothel held the girl's plait from the window. What a shock the prince had when he got to the top! Screeching angrily, the witch flew at him, scratching and clawing, and flung him from the tower. He fell into the thornbushes that grew at its base, and they blinded him. Walking off in shock, he spent two horrible days in the desert, and it was there, on the third day, that Rapunzel found him. She burst out crying when she saw he was blind, and as the tears fell on his eyes, they magically healed them and he could see again. Rejoicing, he led Rapunzel back to his castle where they were soon married.

And Gothel? Some say she was trapped in that tower for the rest of her days. And serve her right.

HOW TO KNIT
Rapunzel

Blessed with an enchanting voice, not to mention those flowing blond locks, Rapunzel seems to have it all. But her sad and lonely childhood tells a different story. So when a prince heard her singing, how could she resist his attention? Knitted here in shades of pink and lilac, Rapunzel has a long plait that can hang down or be wound around her head in a traditional European style.

YOU WILL NEED

2 g/¹⁄₁₆ oz (5 m/5½ yd) white DK yarn
11 g/³⁄₈ oz (27 m/30 yd) flesh DK yarn
3 g/¹⁄₈ oz (7 m/8 yd) deep pink DK yarn
5 g/¹⁄₄ oz (12 m/13 yd) light ochre DK yarn
2 g/¹⁄₁₆ oz (5 m/5½ yd) lilac DK yarn
2 g/¹⁄₁₆ oz (5 m/5½ yd) silver crochet yarn
A small amount of black DK yarn
A very small amount of red DK yarn
One medium size deep pink button
Two 10-mm/³⁄₈-in silver star sequins
White sewing thread
10–15 g/³⁄₈–½ oz polyester toy filling
Red colouring pencil

Use size 3 mm (US 2/3) knitting needles, except when instructed to use size 2.75 mm (US 2) knitting needles.

DOLL

HEAD & BODY
The head and body are knitted together from the base of the body upwards, and include the underpants and top.

Front
Make 1
※ Cast on 14 sts in white.
※ Work 7 rows in st st, beg with a K row.
※ Next row: K.
※ Break white yarn and join deep pink yarn.
※ Work 13 rows in st st, beg with a K row.
※ Next row: K.
※ Break deep pink yarn and join flesh yarn.
※ Next row: K.
※ Next row: (p2tog) twice, P to last 4 sts, (p2tog) twice. [10 sts]
※ Next row: K2, inc1 into next 5 sts, K3. [15 sts]
※ Next row: P.
※ Next row: K1, inc1, K to last 3 sts, inc1, K2. [17 sts]
※ Next row: P.*
※ Rep last 2 rows 3 times more. [23 sts]
※ Work 2 rows in st st, beg with a K row.

* Next row: K2, (k2tog) twice, K11, (ssk) twice, K2. [19 sts]
* Next row: p2tog, P to last 2 sts, p2tog. [17 sts]
* Next row: K2, (k2tog) twice, K5, (ssk) twice, K2. [13 sts]
* Next row: p2tog, P to last 2 sts, p2tog. [11 sts]
* Cast off.

Back
Make 1
* Work as for front to *.
* Next row: K1, inc1, K to last 3 sts, inc1, K1. [19 sts]
* Next row: P.
* Break flesh yarn and join light ochre yarn.
* Next row: K1, inc1, K to last 3 sts, inc1, K1. [21 sts]
* Next row: P.
* Rep last 2 rows once more. [23 sts]
* Work 2 rows in st st, beg with a K row.
* Next row: K2, (k2tog) twice, K11, (ssk) twice, K2. [19 sts]
* Next row: p2tog, P to last 2 sts, p2tog. [17 sts]
* Next row: K2, (k2tog) twice, K5, (ssk) twice, K2. [13 sts]
* Next row: p2tog, P to last 2 sts, p2tog. [11 sts]
* Cast off.

LEGS
The feet and legs are knitted as one piece, starting at the sole of the foot.
Make 2
* Cast on 22 sts in flesh.
* Work 4 rows in st st, beg with a K row.
* Next row: K5, cast off 12 sts, K5. [10 sts]
* Work 19 rows in st st, beg with a K row.
* Cast off.

ARMS
The arms are knitted from the shoulder to the hand.
Make 2
* Cast on 9 sts in lilac.
* 1st row: K1, inc1, K to last 3 sts, inc1, K2. [11 sts]
* Next row: P.
* Next row: K2, m1, K to last 2 sts, m1, K1. [13 sts]

* Work 3 rows in st st, beg with a P row.
* Next row: K2, k2tog, K5, ssk, K2. [11 sts]
* Next row: p2tog, P to last 2 sts, p2tog. [9 sts]
* Next row: K2, k2tog, K1, ssk, K2. [7 sts]
* Next row: K.
* Break lilac yarn and join flesh yarn.
* Work 10 rows in st st, beg with a K row.
* Next row: K1, k2tog, K1, ssk, K1. [5 sts]
* Next row: p2tog, P1, p2tog. [3 sts]
* Next row: s1, k2tog, psso. [1 st]
* Break yarn and pull it through rem st.

MAKING UP
With the two head and body pieces right sides together, oversew around the head. Turn the piece right side out and sew the side seams of the body, leaving the lower edge open for stuffing. Stuff the doll and close the gap using mattress stitch.

Fold the legs in half lengthways, right sides together, and oversew the top and lower edge of the feet. Turn right sides out and sew the back seam, using mattress stitch, and stuff.

Fold the arms in half lengthways, right sides together, and oversew around the hand. Turn right sides out and sew the long seam, using mattress stitch. Stuff the top part of the arms lightly.

Sew the arms and legs in place.

Using light ochre yarn, work a few rows of chain stitch at the front of the head for the hair. For the plait, cut twelve 1-m (39-in) lengths of light ochre yarn. Join the centres of the yarn lengths to the left-hand side of the doll's face. Plait the yarn to the ends and secure.

Work two French knots in black yarn for the eyes. Work two circles of chain stitch around each eye, using white yarn. Using a separated strand of black yarn, work five straight stitches above each eye to represent the eyelashes. Work two short rows of chain stitch in flesh yarn for the nose.

Work a V shape for the mouth in red yarn.

Using silver crochet thread, sew the two star sequins in position to represent earrings. Colour the cheeks, using the red colouring pencil.

SKIRT OF DRESS
Make 2 pieces
* Cast on 22 sts in lilac.
* 1st row: K1, (yf, k2tog) to last st, K1.
* Work 5 rows in st st, beg with a P row.
* Leave lilac yarn at side and join deep pink yarn.
* K 2 rows.
* Break deep pink yarn and work remainder of skirt in lilac.
* Work 2 rows in st st, beg with a K row.
* Next row: K2, k2tog, K to last 4 sts, ssk, K2. [20 sts]
* Work 3 rows in st st, beg with a P row.
* Rep last 4 rows 3 times more. [14 sts]
* Work 2 rows in st st, beg with a K row.
* Cast off pwise.

MAKING UP
Join the side seams using mattress stitch. Oversew the waist in place. Sew the button in position at the neck.

SHOES
Make 2
* Using size 2.75 mm (US 2) needles, cast on 8 sts in silver crochet yarn.
* 1st row: inc1, K to last 2 sts, inc1, K1. [10 sts]
* Next row: P.
* Rep last 2 rows once more. [12 sts]
* Work 2 rows in st st, beg with a K row.
* Next row: inc1, K to last 2 sts, inc1, K1. [14 sts]
* Next row: P5, cast off 4 sts pwise, P to end. Turn work and cont on these last 5 sts only, leaving rem sts on needle or on a safety pin.
* Work 6 rows in st st, beg with a K row.
* Cast off.
* With rs facing, rejoin yarn to rem sts.
* Work 6 rows in st st, beg with a K row.
* Cast off.

MAKING UP
Fold the shoe pieces in half lengthways with the right side facing inward. Oversew the back and lower seam of the shoes. Turn the right way out. Put the shoes on the doll and secure with a couple of stitches. Work a couple of large straight stitches across the foot in a cross shape.

HOW TO KNIT
Dame Gothel

Mean-spirited, ugly, jealous, vindictive . . . I could go on. Dame Gothel is a very nasty piece of work indeed. But in the world of make-believe, we know that characters like the dame normally get their comeuppance. With her wild black hair and clothes that she thinks make her look gorgeous, Dame Gothel is every inch the perfect fairy-tale villain.

YOU WILL NEED

7.5 g/¼ oz (18 m/20 yd) flesh DK yarn

2 g/¹⁄₁₆ oz (4.5 m/5 yd) pale pink DK yarn

2.5 g/¹⁄₁₆ oz (6 m/7 yd) mid-brown DK yarn

3 g/⅛ oz (7.5 m/8½ yd) dark purple DK yarn

3.5 g/⅛ oz (8 m/9 yd) black mohair yarn

4.5 g/⅛ oz (11 m/12 yd) aqua DK yarn

4 g/⅛ oz (9.5 m/10½ yd) mid-pink DK yarn

12 g/½ oz (30 m/33 yd) teal DK yarn

Very small amounts of white, black, bright red and camel DK yarns

One small turquoise button

One snap fastener

Sewing thread

Use size 3 mm (US 2/3) knitting needles, except when instructed to use size 2.75 mm (US 2) knitting needles.

DOLL

HEAD

The head is knitted from the base of the chin to the top of the forehead.
Make 2 pieces
※ Cast on 4 sts in flesh.
※ 1st row: (inc1, K1) twice. [6 sts]
※ Next row: P.
※ Next row: K1, m1, K to last st, m1, K1. [8 sts]
※ Next row: P.
※ Rep last 2 rows 3 times more. [14 sts]
※ Work 10 rows in st st, beg with a K row.
※ Next row: K2, k2tog, K6, ssk, K2. [12 sts]
※ Next row: p2tog, P to last 2 sts, p2tog. [10 sts]
※ Cast off.

NOSE

Make 1
※ Cast on 6 sts in flesh.
※ Work 2 rows in st st, beg with a K row.
※ Next row: k2tog, K2, ssk. [4 sts]
※ Work 3 rows in st st, beg with a P row.
※ Next row: k2tog, ssk. [2 sts]
※ Work 3 rows in st st, beg with a P row.
※ Next row: k2tog. Break yarn and pull through rem st.

BODY

The body is knitted from the lower edge to the neck edge.
Make 2 pieces
※ Cast on 12 sts in pale pink.
※ Work 8 rows in st st, beg with a K row.
※ Next row: K2, k2tog, K4, ssk, K2. [10 sts]
※ Next row: K.
※ Break pale pink yarn and join mid-brown yarn.
※ Work 6 rows in st st, beg with a K row.
※ Next row: K2, m1, K6, m1, K2. [12 sts]
※ Work 7 rows in st st, beg with a P row.
※ Next row; Cast off 1 st, K to end. [11 sts]
※ Next row: Cast off 1 st pwise, P to end. [10 sts]
※ Cast off.

LEGS

The boots and legs are knitted as one piece, starting at the sole of the foot.
Make 2
※ Cast on 26 sts in dark purple.
※ Work 4 rows in st st, beg with a K row.
※ Next row: K5, cast off 16 sts, K to end. [10 sts]
※ Work 8 rows in st st, beg with a P row.
※ K 3 rows.
※ Break dark purple yarn and join flesh yarn.
※ Work 12 rows in st st, beg with a K row.
※ Cast off.

ARMS

The arms are knitted from the top of the shoulder to the tip of the hand.
Make 2
※ Cast on 9 sts in mid-brown.
※ Work 13 rows in st st, beg with a K row.
※ Next row: K.
※ Break mid-brown yarn and join flesh yarn.
※ Work 4 rows in st st, beg with a K row.
※ Next row: K2, k2tog, K1, ssk, K2. [7 sts]
※ Next row: p2tog, P3, p2tog. [5 sts]
※ Next row: k2tog, K1, ssk. [3 sts]
※ Break yarn and thread through rem sts.

MAKING UP

Place the two head pieces right sides together and oversew around the edges, leaving the top of the head open for turning and stuffing. Turn the head right side out, stuff and close the gap using mattress stitch. Sew the body together using mattress stitch, leaving the lower edge open for turning and stuffing. Stuff and close the gap. Sew the head to the body.

Fold one leg in half lengthways, right sides together, and oversew the top and lower edge of the boot. Turn the leg right side out and sew the back seam using mattress stitch. Repeat for the second leg. Stuff the legs and boots.

Fold one arm in half lengthways, right sides together, and oversew around the

hand. Turn the arm right side out and sew the long seam using mattress stitch. Repeat with the second arm. The arms do not need stuffing.

Sew the arms and legs in place.

Cut the black mohair yarn into 25-cm (10-in) lengths and gather together in a bunch. Secure the centre of the lengths to the top of the head and at each side of the face. Trim the lengths if necessary.

Work two French knots in black yarn for the eyes. Work a circle of chain stitch around each eye, using white yarn. Fold the nose piece in half lengthways and oversew in position. Using camel yarn, work a few French knots on the face to represent warts.

Divide a short length of bright red yarn into two thinner strands. Work two straight stitches at an angle, one over the top of the other, for the mouth.

* Next row: k2tog. [1 st]
* Break yarn and pull it through rem st.
* With ws facing, rejoin yarn to rem sts on needle.
* Next row: p2tog, P1. [2 sts]
* Work 3 rows in st st, beg with a K row.
* Next row: p2tog. [1 st]
* Break yarn and pull it through rem st.

MAKING UP

With wrong sides together, join the side seams of the dress using mattress stitch and matching yarns. Join the front to the back at the shoulders.

CLOAK

The cloak is knitted in one piece from the neck edge downwards.
Make 1
* Cast on 28 sts in teal.
* K 2 rows.
* Next row: K2, P5, K1. Turn work and cont on these 8 sts only, leaving rem sts on needle.
* Next row: K.
* Next row: K2, P5, K1.
* Rep these 2 rows 3 times more.
* Break yarn and join it to rem sts on ws of work.
* Next row: K1, P10, K1. Turn work and cont on these 12 sts only, leaving rem sts on needle.
* Next row: K.
* Next row: K1, P10, K1.
* Rep these 2 rows 3 times more.
* Break yarn and join it to rem 8 sts on ws of work.
* Next row: K1, P5, K2.

* Next row: K.
* Rep last 2 rows 3 times more.
* Next row: K1, P5, K2.
* Now work across all 28 sts.
* Next row: K.
* Next row: K2, P to last 2 sts, K2.
* Next row: K6, m1, K4, m1, K8, m1, K4, m1, K6. [32 sts]
* Next row: K2, P to last 2 sts, K2.
* Next row: K.
* Next row: K2, P to last 2 sts, K2.
* Next row: K7, m1, K4, m1, K10, m1, K4, m1, K7. [36 sts]
* Next row: K2, P to last 2 sts, K2.
* Next row: (K2, m1) to last 2 sts, K2. [53 sts]
* Next row: K2, P to last 2 sts, K2.
* Next row: K.
* Rep last 2 rows 10 times more.
* K 4 rows.
* Cast off.

MAKING UP

Sew the button onto the right side of the coat. Sew the top of the snap fastener under the button and the bottom of the snap fastener on the corresponding part of the other side of the cloak.

DRESS

Make 2 pieces
* Using size 3.75 mm (US 5) needles, cast on 16 sts in aqua.
* 1st row: P.
* Next row: K1, (yf, k2tog) to last st, K1.
* Work 13 rows in st st, beg with a P row.
* Break aqua yarn and join mid-pink yarn.
* K 2 rows.
* Next row: K1, k2tog, K to last 3 sts, ssk, K1. [14 sts]
* Work 3 rows in st st, beg with a P row.
* Rep last 4 rows once more. [12 sts]
* Next row: Cast off 2 sts, K2 (3 sts on needle after casting off), cast off 2 sts, K to end. [8 sts]
* Turn and work on 5 sts just knitted only, keeping other sts on needle.
* Next row: Cast off 2 sts pwise, P to end. [3 sts]
* Next row: k2tog, K1. [2 sts]
* Work 3 rows in st st, beg with a P row.

HOW TO KNIT
Rapunzel's Prince

Handsome, gallant, love-struck – and also a prince. It is not hard to see why Rapunzel found this young man so attractive. Sporting a snug red jacket and boots suitable for a lot of woodland walking, he was prepared to go to the ends of the earth for her, whatever obstacles were put in his way. We are sure that you will fall in love with this prince, too.

YOU WILL NEED

11 g/⅜ oz (27 m/30 yd) beige DK yarn

1.5 g/¹⁄₁₆ oz (3 m/3½ yd) black DK yarn

9 g/⅜ oz (22 m/24 yd) red DK yarn

6.5 g/¼ oz (16 m/17½ yd) chestnut brown DK yarn

8 g/¼ oz (19 m/21 yd) caramel DK yarn

Small amount of deep yellow DK yarn

Very small amounts of white and dark red DK yarns

Very small amount of gold crochet yarn

Three 4-mm/⅛-in gold beads

Sewing thread

10–15 g/⅜–½ oz polyester toy filling

Red colouring pencil

Use size 3 mm (US 2/3) knitting needles, except when instructed to use size 2.75 mm (US 2) knitting needles.

DOLL

HEAD
Front
Make 1
* Cast on 12 sts in beige.
* 1st row: K1, inc1, K to last 3 sts, inc1, K2. [14 sts]
* Next row: P.
* Next row: K2, m1, K to last 2 sts, m1, K2. [16 sts]*
* Work 13 rows in st st, beg with a P row.
* Next row: K2, k2tog, K to last 4 sts, ssk, K2. [14 sts]
* Next row: p2tog, P to last 2 sts, p2tog. [12 sts]
* Rep last 2 rows once more. [8 sts]
* Cast off.

Back
Make 1
* Work as for front to *.
* Work 11 rows in st st, beg with a P row.
* Break beige yarn and join black yarn.
* Work 2 rows in st st, beg with a K row.
* Next row: K2, k2tog, K to last 4 sts, ssk, K2. [14 sts]
* Next row: p2tog, P to last 2 sts, p2tog. [12 sts]
* Rep last 2 rows once more. [8 sts]
* Cast off.

EARS
Make 2
* Using size 2.75 mm (US 2) needles, cast on 4 sts in beige.
* 1st row: (k2tog) twice. [2 sts]
* Next row: p2tog.
* Break yarn and pull it through rem st.

BODY
Make 2 pieces
Cast on 14 sts in beige.
* Work 20 rows in st st, beg with a K row.
* Next row: Cast off 1 st, K to end. [13 sts]
* Next row: Cast off 1 st pwise, P to end. [12 sts]
* Cast off.

LEGS
The feet and legs are knitted in one piece, starting at the sole of the foot.
Make 2
* Cast on 26 sts in beige.
* Work 4 rows in st st, beg with a K row.
* Next row: K6, cast off 14 sts, K to end. [12 sts]
* Work 25 rows in st st, beg with a P row.
* Cast off.

ARMS
The arms are knitted from the shoulder to the hand.
Make 2
* Cast on 10 sts in red.
* Work 18 rows in st st, beg with a K row.
* Leave red yarn at the side and join deep yellow yarn.
* K 2 rows. Break deep yellow yarn.
* K 2 rows in red yarn.
* Break red yarn and join beige yarn.
* Work 2 rows in st st, beg with a K row.
* Next row: K2, k2tog, K2, ssk, K2. [8 sts]
* Next row: p2tog, P to last 2 sts, p2tog. [6 sts]
* Cast off.

MAKING UP
Place the two head pieces right sides together and oversew around the edges, leaving the top of the head open for turning and stuffing. Turn the head right side out, stuff and close the gap using mattress stitch. Sew the ears in place. Sew the body together using mattress stitch, leaving the lower edge open for turning and stuffing. Stuff and close the gap. Sew the head to the body.

Fold one leg in half lengthways, right sides together, and oversew the top and lower edge of the feet. Turn the leg right side out and sew the back seam using mattress stitch. Repeat for the second leg. Stuff the legs and feet.

Fold one arm in half lengthways, right sides together, and oversew around the hand. Turn the arm right side out and sew the long seam, using mattress stitch. Repeat for the second arm. The arms do not need stuffing.

Sew the arms and legs in place.

Using black yarn, work a few rows of chain stitch at the front of the head for the hair, using the photograph as a guide (see page 35).

Work two French knots in black yarn for the eyes. Work two circles of chain stitch around each eye, using white yarn. Work two short rows of chain stitch in flesh yarn for the nose.

Using dark red yarn, work two straight stitches side by side for the mouth, so that they form a flattened V shape. Colour the cheeks using a red colouring pencil.

JACKET FRONT & BACK
The two front sides and the back of the jacket are knitted as one piece, from the lower edge to the neck edge. The sleeves have been knitted as part of the doll.
Make 1
* Cast on 30 sts in red.
* K 2 rows.
* Next and every ws row: K2, P to last 2 sts, K2.
* Work 20 rows in st st, beg with a K row, remembering to K2 sts at beg and end of every ws row.
* Next row: K8, turn and work on these sts only, leaving rem sts on needle.
* Next row: P6, K2.
* Next row: K.
* Next row: P6, K2.
* Rep last 2 rows once more.
* Next row: K.
* Break yarn and leave sts on needle.
* On rs of work, join yarn to rem sts.
* Next row: K14.
* Turn and work on these 14 sts only.
* Work 6 rows in st st, beg with a P row.
* Break yarn and transfer sts onto right-hand needle without knitting them.
* On rs of work, join yarn to rem 8 sts on left-hand needle.
* Next row: K.
* Next row: K2, P6.
* Next row: K.
* Rep last 2 rows twice more.
* Now work across all 30 sts on needle.

* Next row: Cast off 2 sts kwise, P7 [8 sts on needle, including rem st from casting off], (p2tog) twice, P2, (p2tog) twice, P to last 2 sts, K2. [24 sts]
* Next row: Cast off 2 sts, K to end. [22 sts]
* K 2 rows.
* Cast off.

BELT

Make 1

* Cast on 30 sts in chestnut brown.
* Work 2 rows in st st, beg with a K row.
* Cast off pwise.

MAKING UP

Put the jacket on the doll and oversew the armhole edges around the top of the arms. Overlap the jacket fronts and sew the three gold beads in place on the right-hand front of the jacket. Fasten the jacket by using the gaps between stitches on the left-hand front for buttonholes. Oversew the short edges of the belt. Position on the doll. Using doubled gold crochet yarn, work a series of straight stitches to form a square shape to represent a buckle in the centre of the belt.

TROUSERS

The trousers are knitted as one piece.
Make 1

* Cast on 14 sts for first leg in caramel.
* K 2 rows.
* Work 23 rows in st st, beg with a P row.
* Break yarn and leave sts on spare needle.
* Work a second trouser leg exactly as the first, but don't break yarn.
* Next row: K14 sts from second trouser leg, then knit across 14 sts from first trouser leg. [28 sts]
* Work 9 rows in st st, beg with a P row.
* Next row: (K1, P1) to end.
* Rep last row once more.
* Cast off quite loosely, keeping to the K1, P1 pattern.

MAKING UP

Using mattress stitch, join the back seam so that the lowest part of the seam is level with the crotch. Then join the two inside leg seams, again using mattress stitch.

BOOTS

Make 2

* Cast on 28 sts in chestnut brown.
* K 2 rows.
* Work 4 rows in st st, beg with a K row.
* Next row: K8, cast off 12 sts, K to end. [16 sts]
* Work 10 rows in st st, beg with a P row.
* Next row: K.
* Cast off pwise loosely.

MAKING UP

Fold the pieces in half widthways, right sides together. Oversew the lower and upper seams of the foot. Then turn the boots right side out and sew the back seams using mattress stitch.

Hansel & Gretel

Hansel and Gretel were twins: bright, brave and very close to one another. Sadly, their mother died when they were young, and when their father remarried he chose badly. Their new stepmother was very jealous of his children. Their father was a poor woodcutter and the stepmother constantly urged him to take the children miles into the wood and leave them there – **"We're too poor to feed them; it's kinder not to watch them starve . . ."** Weak-willed as he was, he gave in to her and took the children deep into the forest and left them there.

Hansel was no fool. He was suspicious about the long walk, and when their father disappeared, he showed Gretel that he had left a trail of little white pebbles to lead them back home. How angry the stepmother was when they trotted in the door! And the very next day, she nagged the woodcutter into taking them for another long walk into the forest. This time, Hansel had no pebbles, only a slice of bread. He left a trail of crumbs, but when his father disappeared again and he looked for them to follow, he found that the birds had eaten them up.

"Cheer up, Hansel," said his sister, who was also full of spirit. **"Let's walk on for a while and see what we can find."** And after fully two hours of walking, the twins arrived at a very peculiar and wonderful house indeed.

The roof and the walls were made of gingerbread – not the dry, hard sort, but the soft and delicious kind that's decorated with icing. Candy drops were set into the icing, and the windows were made from tasty-looking barley sugar and golden butterscotch. Both hungry twins broke off big chunks of cake and began to eat.

But . . . **"Who's munching on my house?"** came a shrill voice, and an old lady hobbled out of the house. The children stared – who would have thought that such a gorgeous cottage would belong to such a shabby creature? Seemingly friendly, she invited them in. Inside the house, though, it was a different story. True, the table was covered with cakes and other rich foods, but before they had had time to look around properly, the witch (for so the old lady was) had roughly thrust Hansel into a large iron cage in the corner and turned the lock on him. **"Ha!"** she jeered. **"I'm sick of sweet things. I'm going to feed you every day and when you grow fat, I will turn you into a meaty stew. You"**, turning to Gretel, **"will do the housework."** How scared they were! But they were resourceful, and they were sure they could find a way out before Hansel was eaten. The key to the cage was on a string around the witch's neck, and she kept a sharp eye on them. Every day, she fed Hansel sweet things and asked to feel his finger so that she could tell how fat he was getting because her eyesight was poor. Hansel stuck out a finger of barley sugar instead of his own, and the witch grew irritable when he didn't put on weight. Finally, **"Heat up the oven,"** she told Gretel. **"I'm going to eat him anyway!"** Gretel saw her chance, **"Please,"** she cried, sticking her head in the oven, **"It seems very hot, but I can't really tell."** Huffing and puffing, the witch leant into the oven. Quick as a flash, Gretel seized the string with the key with one hand and gave the witch a push with the other. The nasty old thing fell into the flames and was burned to death.

And the twins? Filling a bag with the witch's treasure, they ran through the forest until they found their way back to their father's house. When they arrived, they found that their stepmother had died while they were away. Their father cried with joy to have his children back. And they all lived together happily ever after.

Hansel

Hansel is a dapper little fellow. Dressed in a pair of striking emerald green shorts, red jersey and royal blue stockings, he also has a deep brown hat that sets his outfit off a treat. As you will discover in the story, this lad is more than just a pretty face. He is also street smart – and really protective of his twin sister, Gretel.

HANSEL

YOU WILL NEED

2 g/¹⁄₁₆ oz (4 m/4 ½ yd) white DK yarn

4.5 g/⅛ oz (11 m/12 yd) red DK yarn

2.5 g/¹⁄₁₆ oz (5.5 m/6 yd) flesh DK yarn

1.5 g/¹⁄₁₆ oz (3 m/3½ yd) mid-yellow DK yarn

2.5 g/¹⁄₁₆ oz (5.5 m/6 yd) dark brown DK yarn

2 g/¹⁄₁₆ oz (4.5 m/5 yd) royal blue DK yarn

5.5 g/¼ oz (13 m/14½ yd) emerald green DK yarn

Very small amounts of black and deep pink DK yarns

Two small white buttons

Red sewing thread

10–15 g/⅜–½ oz polyester toy filling

Red colouring pencil

Use size 3 mm (US 2/3) knitting needles.

DOLL

BODY & HEAD
The body and head are knitted together from the base of the body upwards, and include the underpants and jersey.

Front
Make 1

❋ Cast on 13 sts in white.

❋ Work 7 rows in st st, beg with a K row.

❋ Next row: K.

❋ Break white yarn and join red yarn.

❋ Work 13 rows in st st, beg with a K row.

❋ Next row: K.

❋ Break red yarn and join flesh yarn.

❋ Next row: K.

❋ Next row: (p2tog) twice, P to last 4 sts, (p2tog) twice. [9 sts]

❋ Next row: K1, inc1 into next 6 sts, K2. [15 sts]

❋ Next row: P.

* Next row: K1, inc1, K to last 3 sts, inc1, K2. [17 sts]
* Next row: P. *
* Rep last 2 rows twice more. [21 sts]
* Work 2 rows in st st, beg with a K row.
* Next row: K2, (k2tog) twice, K9, (ssk) twice, K2. [17 sts]
* Next row: p2tog, P to last 2 sts, p2tog. [15 sts]
* Next row: K2, (k2tog) twice, K3, (ssk) twice, K2. [11 sts]
* Next row: p2tog, P to last 2 sts, p2tog. [9 sts]
* Cast off.

Back
Make 1
* Work as for front to *.
* Break flesh yarn and join mid-yellow yarn.
* Next row: K1, inc1, K to last 3 sts, inc1, K2. [19 sts]
* Next row: P.
* Rep last 2 rows once more. [21 sts]
* Work 2 rows in st st, beg with a K row.
* Next row: K2, (k2tog) twice, K9, (ssk) twice, K2. [17 sts]
* Next row: p2tog, P to last 2 sts, p2tog. [15 sts]
* Next row: K2, (k2tog) twice, K3, (ssk) twice, K2. [11 sts]
* Next row: p2tog, P to last 2 sts, p2tog. [9 sts]
* Cast off.

LEGS
The boots and legs are knitted as one piece, starting at the sole of the boot.
Make 2
* Cast on 20 sts in dark brown.
* Work 4 rows in st st, beg with a K row.
* Next row: K5, cast off 10 sts, K5. [10 sts]
* Work 4 rows in st st, beg with a P row.
* Next row: K.
* Break dark brown yarn and join royal blue yarn.
* Work 12 rows in st st, beg with a K row.
* Cast off.

ARMS
The arms are knitted from the shoulder to the hand.
Make 2
* Cast on 7 sts in red.
* Work 19 rows in st st, beg with a K row.
* Next row: K.
* Break red yarn and join flesh yarn.
* Work 2 rows in st st, beg with a K row.
* Next row: K1, k2tog, K1, ssk, K1. [5 sts]
* Next row: p2tog, P1, p2tog. [3 sts]
* Next row: s1, k2tog, psso. [1 st]
* Break yarn and pull it through rem st.

MAKING UP
With the two head and body pieces right sides together, oversew around the head. Turn the piece right side out and sew the side seams of the body using mattress stitch, leaving the lower edge open for stuffing. Stuff the doll and close the gap using mattress stitch.

Fold one leg in half lengthways, right sides together, and oversew the top and lower edge of the boots. Turn the leg right side out and sew the back seam using mattress stitch. Repeat for the second leg. Stuff the legs and boots.

Fold one arm in half lengthways, right sides together, and oversew around the hand. Turn the arm right side out and sew the long seams of the jersey using mattress stitch. Repeat for the second arm. The arms do not need stuffing.

Sew the arms and legs in place.

Using mid-yellow yarn, work a few rows of chain stitch at the front of the head for the hair.

Work two French knots in black yarn for the eyes. Work two circles of chain stitch around each eye, using white yarn. Work two short rows of chain stitch in flesh yarn for the nose.

Divide a short length of deep pink yarn into two thinner strands. Work two straight stitches, one over the top of the other, for the mouth. Colour the cheeks using a red colouring pencil.

SHORTS
The shorts are knitted as one piece.
Make 1
* Cast on 16 sts in emerald green.
* Work 7 rows in st st, beg with a P row.
* Break yarn and leave sts on a spare needle or stitch holder.
* Work a second trouser leg exactly as the first, but don't break yarn.
* Next row: K16 sts from second trouser leg, then knit across 16 sts from first trouser leg. [32 sts]
* Work 8 rows in st st, beg with a P row.
* K 2 rows.
* Cast off quite loosely.

STRAPS
Make 2
* Cast on 24 sts in emerald green.
* Cast off kwise.

MAKING UP
Using mattress stitch, join the back seam of the shorts so that the lowest part of the seam is level with the crotch. Then join the two inside leg seams, again using mattress stitch. Put the shorts on the doll and sew the straps in place, crossing them at the back. Sew the buttons to the front of the straps, as shown in the photograph.

CAP

Make 1

❋ Cast on 28 sts in dark brown.

❋ K 2 rows.

❋ Next row: P.

❋ Next row: K1, (m1, K1) to end.
  [55 sts]

❋ Next row: P.

❋ Next row: K.

❋ Next row: Cast off 23 sts, K9, cast off
  23 sts. [9 sts]

❋ Break yarn and rejoin it to rs of 9 sts
  just worked.

❋ Next row: K1, m1, K to last st, m1, K1.
  [11 sts]

❋ Next row: P.

❋ Rep last 2 rows 4 times more. [19 sts]

❋ Next row: K1, k2tog, K to last 3 sts,
  ssk, K1. [17 sts]

❋ Next row: P.

❋ Rep last 2 rows 3 times more. [11 sts]

❋ Next row: K1, k2tog, K to last 3 sts,
  ssk, K1. [9 sts]

❋ Cast off pwise.

PEAK

Make 1

❋ With rs facing, pick up and K 9 sts
  across the centre of the front of the hat.

❋ Next row: P.

❋ Next row: k2tog, K5, ssk. [7 sts]

❋ Next row: p2tog, P3, p2tog. [5 sts]

❋ Next row: inc1, K to last 2 sts, inc1,
  K1. [7 sts]

❋ Next row: inc1 pwise, P to last 2 sts,
  inc1 pwise, P1. [9 sts]

❋ Cast off loosely.

MAKING UP

Join the back seam of the side band of
the hat. Oversew the top of the hat to the
side band, working from the inside. Fold
the second part of the peak (which will
become the lining) upwards, so that the
right sides of the peak are together.
Oversew the sides. Turn the peak right
side out and oversew the edge of the
peak facing in place at the inside.

HOW TO KNIT
Gretel

Gretel is probably the most adorable little girl in the world of fairy tales. Here, she is cutely dressed in a charming folk dress in rich royal blue with a pair of contrasting bright red stockings. Her hair is arranged in practical plaits and her expression is understandably slightly nervous. She'd like to smile – if only life was a little bit kinder.

GRETEL
YOU WILL NEED

3 g/⅛ oz (6.5 m/7 yd) white DK yarn
4 g/⅛ oz (9 m/10 yd) royal blue DK yarn
4 g/⅛ oz (9 m/10 yd) flesh DK yarn
1.5 g/¹⁄₁₆ oz (3.5 m/4 yd) mid-brown DK yarn
4 g/⅛ oz (9.5 m/10½ yd) red DK yarn
1 g/¹⁄₁₆ oz (1.5 m/2 yd) emerald green DK yarn
2 g/¹⁄₁₆ oz (5 m/5½ yd) dark brown DK yarn
Small amount of black DK yarn
Very small amount of deep pink DK yarn
10–15 g/⅜–½ oz polyester toy filling
Red colouring pencil

Use size 3 mm (US 2/3) knitting needles, except when instructed to use size 2.75 mm (US 2) knitting needles.

DOLL

BODY & HEAD
The body and head are knitted together from the base of the body upwards and include the underpants and bodice of the dress.

Front
Make 1
❋ Cast on 13 sts in white.
❋ Work 7 rows in st st, beg with a K row.
❋ Next row: K.
❋ Break white yarn and join royal blue yarn.
❋ Work 11 rows in st st, beg with a K row.
❋ Next row: K.
❋ Break royal blue yarn and join flesh yarn.
❋ Next row: K.
❋ Next row: (p2tog) twice, P to last 4 sts, (p2tog) twice. [9 sts]
❋ Next row: K1, inc1 into next 6 sts, K2. [15 sts]
❋ Next row: P.

❋ Next row: K1, inc1, K to last 3 sts, inc1, K2. [17 sts]
❋ Next row: P. *
❋ Rep last 2 rows twice more. [21 sts]
❋ Work 2 rows in st st, beg with a K row.
❋ Next row: K2, (k2tog) twice, K9, (ssk) twice, K2. [17 sts]
❋ Next row: p2tog, P to last 2 sts, p2tog. [15 sts]
❋ Next row: K2, (k2tog) twice, K3, (ssk) twice, K2. [11 sts]
❋ Next row: p2tog, P to last 2 sts, p2tog. [9 sts]
❋ Cast off.

Back
Make 1
❋ Work as for front to *.
❋ Break flesh yarn and join mid-brown yarn.
❋ Next row: K1, inc1, K to last 3 sts, inc1, K2. [19 sts]
❋ Next row: P.
❋ Rep last 2 rows once more. [21 sts]
❋ Work 2 rows in st st, beg with a K row.
❋ Next row: K2, (k2tog) twice, K9, (ssk) twice, K2. [17 sts]

❋ Next row: p2tog, P to last 2 sts, p2tog. [15 sts]
❋ Next row: K2, (k2tog) twice, K3, (ssk) twice, K2. [11 sts]
❋ Next row: p2tog, P to last 2 sts, p2tog. [9 sts]
❋ Cast off.

LEGS
The feet and legs are knitted as one piece, starting at the sole of the foot.
Make 2
❋ Cast on 20 sts in red.
❋ Work 4 rows in st st, beg with a K row.
❋ Next row: K5, cast off 10 sts, K5. [10 sts]
❋ Work 15 rows in st st, beg with a P row.
❋ Cast off.

ARMS
The arms are knitted from the shoulder to the hand.
Make 2
❋ Cast on 7 sts in royal blue.
❋ Work 7 rows in st st, beg with a K row.
❋ Next row: K.

❋ Next row: P.
❋ Break royal blue yarn and join flesh yarn.
❋ Work 11 rows in st st, beg with a P row.
❋ Next row: K1, k2tog, K1, ssk, K1. [5 sts]
❋ Next row: p2tog, P1, p2tog. [3 sts]
❋ Next row: s1, k2tog, psso. [1 st]
❋ Break yarn and pull it through rem st.

MAKING UP

With the two head and body pieces right sides together, oversew around the head. Turn the piece right side out and sew the side seams of the body, leaving the lower edge open for stuffing. Stuff the doll and close the gap using mattress stitch.

Fold one leg in half lengthways, right sides together, and oversew the top and lower edge of the foot. Turn the leg right side out and sew the back seams, using mattress stitch. Repeat for the second leg. Stuff the legs and feet.

Fold one arm in half lengthways, right sides together, and oversew around the hand. Turn the arm right side out and sew the long seam, using mattress stitch. Repeat for the second arm. The arms do not need stuffing.

Sew the arms and legs in place.

Split a length of red yarn into two thinner strands and use one of these to embroider two cross shapes on the front of the bodice, as shown in the photograph (see page 44).

Using light brown yarn, work a few rows of chain stitch at the front of the head for the hair, using the photograph as a guide. For the plaits, cut six 35-cm (14-in) lengths of light brown yarn. Thread three lengths through one corner of the head so that you have six shorter lengths. Divide these shorter lengths into three groups of two strands and plait them. Use two strands to tie around the bottom of the plait to secure it. Make the second plait in the same way.

Work two French knots in black yarn for the eyes. Work two circles of chain stitch around each eye, using white yarn. Using a single ply of black yarn, work three straight stitches above each eye to represent the eyelashes. Work two short rows of chain stitch in flesh yarn for the nose.

Divide a short length of deep pink yarn into two thinner strands. Work two straight stitches, one over the top of the other, for the mouth. Colour the cheeks using a red colouring pencil.

DRESS SKIRT
Make 1
❋ Cast on 38 sts in royal blue.
❋ Work 3 rows in st st, beg with a P row.
❋ Leave royal blue yarn at side and join emerald green yarn.
❋ K 2 rows. Break emerald green yarn and use royal blue yarn.
❋ Work 10 rows in st st, beg with a K row.
❋ Next row: (k2tog) 9 times, K2, (ssk) 9 times. [20 sts]
❋ K 2 rows.
❋ Cast off.

MAKING UP

Sew the back seam of the skirt using mattress stitch. Oversew the skirt in place around the waist of the doll.

APRON
Make 1
❋ Cast on 12 sts in white leaving a tail approx. 30 cm (12 in) long.
❋ K 2 rows.
❋ Next row: K2, P to last 2 sts, K2.
❋ Next row: K.
❋ Next row: K2, P to last 2 sts, K2.
❋ Rep last 2 rows twice more.
❋ Next row: k2tog, K to last 2 sts, ssk. [10 sts]
❋ Rep last row once more. [8 sts]
❋ Cast off pwise, leaving a tail approx. 30 cm (12 in) long.

MAKING UP

Thread the tail from casting off up the side of apron and secure it at the top. Using the two tails, work two crochet chains approximately 7 cm/3 in long for the apron ties.

SHOES
Make 2
❋ Using size 2.75 mm (US 2) needles, cast on 8 sts in dark brown.
❋ 1st row: inc1, K to last 2 sts, inc1, K1. [10 sts]
❋ Next row: P.
❋ Rep last 2 rows once more. [12 sts]
❋ Work 2 rows in st st, beg with a K row.
❋ Next row: inc1, K to last 2 sts, inc1, K1. [14 sts]
❋ Next row: P5, cast off 4 sts pwise, P to end. Turn work and cont on these last 5 sts only, leaving rem sts on needle or on a safety pin.
❋ Work 6 rows in st st, beg with a K row.
❋ Cast off.
❋ With rs facing, rejoin yarn to rem 5 sts.
❋ Work 6 rows in st st, beg with a K row.
❋ Cast off.

MAKING UP

Fold the shoe pieces in half lengthways with the right side facing inward. Oversew the back and lower seam of the shoes. Turn the right way out. Put the shoes on the doll and secure with a couple of stitches. Work a couple of large straight stitches across the foot to represent the bar of the shoe.

HOW TO KNIT
The Wicked Witch

If there is a more gruesome fairy-tale character than this wicked witch in the tale of Hansel and Gretel, then she must be a very bad person indeed. This child-hating old woman, complete with a wonky tooth and warts, is dressed in an ancient shabby dress and drab coat – but she's great fun to knit and the perfect antidote to knitting the sweet-natured Hansel and Gretel.

YOU WILL NEED

6 g/¼ oz (14 m/15½ yd) flesh DK yarn

5 g/¼ oz (12 m/13 yd) grey DK yarn

7 g/¼ oz (17 m/18½ yd) light olive green DK yarn

3 g/⅛ oz (7 m/8 yd) dark brown DK yarn

5 g/¼ oz (12 m/13 yd) brown/green DK yarn

20 g/¾ oz (50 m/55 yd) mid-blue DK yarn

Small amounts of black and white DK yarns

Very small amounts of pink and camel DK yarns

One medium grey button

One snap fastener

White sewing thread

10–15 g/⅜–½ oz polyester toy filling

Use size 3 mm (US 2/3) knitting needles, except when instructed to use size 3.75 mm (US 5) knitting needles.

DOLL

HEAD
The head is knitted from the forehead down to the chin.

Front
Make 1
* Cast on 12 sts in flesh.
* 1st row: inc1, K to last 2 sts, inc1, K1. [14 sts]
* Next row: P.
* Next row: K2, m1, K to last 2 sts, m1, K2. [16 sts]
* Next row: P.*
* Rep last 2 rows once more. [18 sts]
* Work 8 rows in st st, beg with a K row.
* Next row: K2, (k2tog) twice, K to last 6 sts, (ssk) twice, K2. [14 sts]
* Next row: p2tog, P to last 2 sts, p2tog. [12 sts]
* Next row: K2, (k2tog) twice, K to last 6 sts, (ssk) twice, K2. [8 sts]
* Cast off pwise.

Back
Make 1
* Work as for front to *.
* Break flesh yarn and join grey yarn.
* Next row: K2, m1, K to last 2 sts, m1, K2. [18 sts]
* Work 9 rows in st st, beg with a P row.
* Next row: K2, (k2tog) twice, K to last 6 sts, (ssk) twice, K2. [14 sts]
* Next row: p2tog, P to last 2 sts, p2tog. [12 sts]
* Next row: K2, (k2tog) twice, K to last 6 sts, (ssk) twice, K2. [8 sts]
* Cast off pwise.

BODY
The body is knitted from the lower edge to the neck edge. The underpants and top are knitted as part of the body.
Make 2 pieces
* Cast on 22 sts in grey.
* Work 7 rows in st st, beg with a K row.
* Next row: K.
* Break grey yarn and join light olive green yarn.
* Work 10 rows in st st, beg with a K row.

* Next row: K2, k2tog, K to last 4 sts, ssk, K2. [20 sts]
* Next row: P.
* Rep last 2 rows once more. [18 sts]
* Cast off.

LEGS
The boots and legs are knitted as one piece, starting at the sole of the boot.
Make 2
* Cast on 24 sts in dark brown.
* Work 4 rows in st st beg with a K row.
* Next row: K7, cast off 10 sts, K to end. [14 sts]
* Work 4 rows in st st, beg with a P row.
* Next row: K.
* Break dark brown yarn and join flesh yarn.
* Work 12 rows in st st, beg with a K row.
* Cast off loosely.

ARMS
The arms are knitted from the shoulder to the hand.
Make 2
* Cast on 10 sts in light olive green.
* Work 15 rows in st st, beg with a K row.
* Next row: K.
* Break light olive green yarn and join flesh yarn.
* Work 2 rows in st st, beg with a K row.
* Next row: k2tog, K6, ssk. [8 sts]
* Next row: p2tog, P4, p2tog. [6 sts]
* Next row: k2tog, K2, ssk. [4 sts]
* Break yarn, thread it through rem sts and secure.

HAIR
Make 1
* Using size 3.75 mm (US 5) needles, cast on 15 sts in grey.
* 1st row: K, but for every stitch wind the yarn around your needle 3 times instead of the usual once (see Extended Garter stitch, page 11).
* Next row: K each stitch, dropping extra loops.
* Cast off.

MAKING UP
Place the two head pieces right sides together and oversew around the edges, leaving the top of the head open for turning and stuffing. Turn the head right side out, stuff and close the gap using mattress stitch. Sew the body together using mattress stitch, leaving the lower edge open for turning and stuffing. Stuff and close the gap. Sew the head to the body.

Fold one leg in half lengthways, right sides together, and oversew the top and lower edge of the boot. Turn the leg right side out and sew the back seam, using mattress stitch. Repeat for the second leg. Stuff the legs and boots.

Fold one arm in half lengthways, right sides together, and oversew around the hand. Turn the arm right side out and sew the long seam, using mattress stitch. Repeat for the second arm. The arms do not need stuffing.

Sew the arms and legs in place.

Fold the hair strip in half lengthways and oversew it to the top of the head.

Work two French knots in black yarn for the eyes – one high up the face and one lower down. Work a circle of chain stitch around one eye and two circles of chain stitch around the other eye, using white yarn. Using flesh yarn, work a couple of straight stitches at the top of each eye to represent the eyelids. Using flesh yarn, work a flattened coil of chain stitches for the nose. Using camel yarn, work a few French knots to represent warts.

Divide a short length of pink yarn into two thinner strands. Work two straight stitches, one over the top of the other, for the mouth. Using a strand of white yarn, work a couple of small straight stitches, one on top of the other, for the tooth.

TUNIC
Make 2 pieces
* Using size 3.75 mm (US 5) needles, cast on 16 sts in brown/green.
* 1st row: K.

* Next row: K, but for every stitch wind the yarn around your needle twice instead of the usual once (see Extended Garter stitch, page 11).
* Next row: K each stitch, dropping extra loops.
* Rep last 2 rows 5 times more.
* Next row: Keeping to the 'stretched' garter stitch technique, k2tog, K to last 2 sts, ssk. [14 sts]
* Next row: K each stitch, dropping extra loops.
* Rep last 2 rows once more. [12 sts]
* Next row: K, but for every stitch wind the yarn around your needle twice instead of the usual once.
* Next row: K each stitch, dropping extra loops.
* Rep last 2 rows twice more.
* Cast off loosely.

MAKING UP

Oversew the tunic together at the shoulders and side seams, leaving enough room for the arms and head.

CLOAK

The main part of the cloak is knitted as one piece from the neck edge downwards. The sleeves and hood are sewn on separately.
Make 1
* Cast on 36 sts in mid-blue.
* K 2 rows.
* Next row: K2, P8. Turn work and cont on these 10 sts only, leaving rem sts on needle.
* Next row: K.
* Next row: K2, P8.
* Rep last 2 rows twice more.
* Break yarn and join it to rem sts on ws of work.
* Next row: P16. Turn work and cont on these 16 sts only, leaving rem sts on needle.
* Work 6 rows in st st, beg with a K row.
* Break yarn and join it to rem 10 sts on ws of work.
* Next row: P8, K2.
* Next row: K.
* Rep these rows twice more.
* Next row: P8, K2.

* Now work across all 36 sts.
* Next row: K8, m1, K4, m1, K12, m1, K4, m1, K8. [40 sts]
* Next and every ws row unless stated: K2, P to last 2 sts, K2.
* Next rs row: K.
* Next rs row: K9, m1, K4, m1, K14, m1, K4, m1, K9. [44 sts]
* Next rs row: K.
* Next row: K.
* K 3 rows.
* Next row: (K2, m1) to last 2 sts, K2. [65 sts]
* Next row: K2, P to last 2 sts, K2.
* Work 13 rows in st st, beg with a K row and knitting 2 sts at the beg and end of every ws row.
* K 4 rows.
* Cast off.

SLEEVES

Make 2
* Cast on 16 sts in mid-blue.
* Work 8 rows in st st, beg with a K row.
* K 2 rows.
* Cast off.

HOOD

The hood is knitted from the face edge to the back.
Make 1
* Cast on 32 sts in mid-blue.
* K 2 rows.
* Work 17 rows in st st, beg with a P row.
* Cast off.

MAKING UP

Sew the seams of the sleeves using mattress stitch. Insert them into the armholes of the cloak and oversew them in place from the inside.

Fold the hood piece in half widthways and sew the back seam. Oversew the hood in place around the neck edge of the coat. The edges of the hood should come 1 cm (½ in) in from the front edges of the cloak.

Sew the button onto the right side of the cloak at the waist. Sew the top of the snap fastener under the button and the bottom of it on the corresponding part of the other side of the cloak.

Goldilocks & the Three Bears

Goldilocks's mother believed in independence, and the little girl was allowed to explore the countryside around her home as she pleased. One day, she wandered further than usual and found herself outside a cottage she had never seen before. It was spick and span and – tempting for a curious little girl – the door was ajar. Goldilocks went straight in, but no one seemed to be there. They clearly weren't far away, because in the kitchen, three chairs were set around a table, and on the table were three bowls of porridge. Goldilocks had walked a long way and was feeling in need of a rest. So she sat down on the biggest chair, but it wasn't comfortable. **"Too hard!"** she cried, switching to the middle-sized chair, which was covered in cushions. **"Too soft!"** she pouted, and moved to the smallest chair, which she found just perfect for her. Then she realized she was hungry, too.

So she dipped a spoon in the biggest bowl of porridge. But it was too hot. On to the middle bowl – but no, that one was too cold. So she tried the small bowl and found it tasted delicious. Adding some honey from a jar on the table, and without thinking that the porridge belonged to someone else, who might be hungry, too, she ate it all up. Now that she'd eaten, Goldilocks felt sleepy. There were three beds in the adjoining bedroom, a large one, a middle-sized one and a small cot. As usual, our heroine tried all three – and, as you'd expect, it was the small one that fitted her the best. So she clambered into the cot and fell fast asleep.

But who owned the cottage? A family of three bears, who had heard of a honey tree and just gone out for an hour. They arrived back, tired and hungry, and sat down around the table to eat. But,
"Who's been sitting in my chair?" growled Daddy Bear, and
"Who's been sitting in MY chair?" shrilled Mother Bear, and
"Who's been sitting in my chair?" squeaked Baby Bear,
"the cushion is all messed up!" And it was the same story when it came to the porridge: **"Who's tried my porridge?"** gruffed Daddy Bear. **"And mine!"** said Mother Bear. **"And mine!"** said Baby Bear. **"And they've eaten it all up!"** At that moment, they heard a

movement from the bedroom. All three rushed next door. **"Who's been in my bed?"** shouted Daddy Bear. **"And mine!"** called Mother Bear. **"And mine!"** cried Baby Bear, **"And she's still there!"** Goldilocks awoke to find three very angry bears staring down at her. Very much frightened, she jumped out of bed and ran out of the cottage and all the way home. And these days, she's less inclined to use other people's things without asking first.

HOW TO KNIT
Goldilocks

With her tumbling golden hair and demure smile, she looks as if butter wouldn't melt in her mouth. Dressed so sweetly in pale green and purple, she looks as if she's the kind of girl who would never put a foot out of line. But looks can be deceptive. Goldilocks is a girl who knows just what she wants. And when she went walking in the wood near her home, she started to feel a little peckish. So why not just slip into that charming little cottage and help herself to a bit of breakfast? No one will care, will they?

YOU WILL NEED

2 g/¹⁄₁₆ oz (4 m/4½ yd) pale pink DK yarn
3.5 g/⅛ oz (8.5 m/9½ yd) pale green DK yarn
6 g/¼ oz (15 m/16½ yd) flesh DK yarn
2 g/¹⁄₁₆ oz (4.5 m/5 yd) deep yellow DK yarn
3 g/⅛ oz (6.5 m/7 yd) white DK yarn
7.5 g/¼ oz (18 m/20 yd) purple DK yarn
2 g/¹⁄₁₆ oz (5 m/5½ yd) red DK yarn
Small amount of black DK yarn
10–15 g (⅜–½ oz) polyester toy filling
Red colouring pencil

Use size 3 mm (US 2/3) knitting needles, except when instructed to use size 2.75 mm (US 2) knitting needles.

DOLL

BODY & HEAD
The body and body are knitted together from the base of the body upwards and include the underpants and top.

Front
Make 1
* Cast on 13 sts in pale pink.
* Work 7 rows in st st, beg with a K row.
* Next row: K.
* Break pale pink yarn and join pale green yarn.
* Work 13 rows in st st, beg with a K row.
* Next row: K.
* Break pale green yarn and join flesh yarn.
* Next row: K.
* Next row: (p2tog) twice, P to last 4 sts, (p2tog) twice. [9 sts]
* Next row: K1, inc1 into next 6 sts, K2. [15 sts]
* Next row: P.
* Next row: K1, inc1, K to last 3 sts, inc1, K2. [17 sts]
* Next row: P.*
* Rep last 2 rows 3 times more. [23 sts]
* Work 2 rows in st st, beg with a K row.
* Next row: K2, (k2tog) twice, K11, (ssk) twice, K2. [19 sts]
* Next row: p2tog, P to last 2 sts, p2tog. [17 sts]

* Next row: K2, (k2tog) twice, K5, (ssk) twice, K2. [13 sts]
* Next row: p2tog, P to last 2 sts, p2tog. [11 sts]
* Cast off.

Back
Make 1
* Work as for front to *.
* Break flesh yarn and join deep yellow yarn.
* Next row: K1, inc1, K to last 3 sts, inc1, K2. [19 sts]
* Next row: P.
* Rep last 2 rows twice more. [23 sts]
* Work 2 rows in st st, beg with a K row.
* Next row: K2, (k2tog) twice, K11, (ssk) twice, K2. [17 sts]
* Next row: p2tog, P to last 2 sts, p2tog. [15 sts]
* Next row: K2, (k2tog) twice, K5, (ssk) twice, K2. [13 sts]
* Next row: p2tog, P to last 2 sts, p2tog. [11 sts]
* Cast off.

LEGS
The socks and legs are knitted as one piece, starting at the sole of the foot.
Make 2
* Cast on 22 sts in white.
* Work 4 rows in st st, beg with a K row.
* Next row: K5, cast off 12 sts, K5. [10 sts]
* Work 6 rows in st st, beg with a P row.
* Next row: K.
* Break white yarn and join flesh yarn.
* Work 10 rows in st st, beg with a K row.
* Cast off.

ARMS
The arms are knitted from the shoulder to the hand.
Make 2
* Cast on 7 sts in pale green.
* Work 7 rows in st st, beg with a K row.
* Next row: K.
* Break pale green yarn and join flesh yarn.
* Work 12 rows in st st, beg with a K row.
* Next row: K1, k2tog, K1, ssk, K1. [5 sts]
* Next row: p2tog, P1, p2tog. [3 sts]
* Next row: s1, k2tog, psso. [1 st]
* Break yarn and pull it through rem st.

MAKING UP
With the two head and body pieces right sides together, oversew around the head. Turn the piece right side out and sew the side seams of the body, leaving the lower edge open for stuffing. Stuff the doll and close the gap using mattress stitch.

Fold the legs in half lengthways, right sides together, and oversew the top and lower edge of the feet. Turn right sides out and sew the back seam, using mattress stitch, and stuff.

Fold the arms in half lengthways, right sides together, and oversew around the hands. Turn right sides out and sew the long seam, using mattress stitch. The arms do not need stuffing.

Sew the arms and legs in place.

Using deep yellow yarn, work a few rows of chain stitch at the front of the head for the hair. Make four 12-cm (4½-in) crochet chains and arrange into loops at each side of the head.

Work two French knots in black yarn for the eyes. Work two circles of chain stitch around each eye, using white yarn. Using a separated strand of black yarn, work three straight stitches above each eye for the eyelashes. Work two short rows of chain stitch in flesh yarn for the nose.

Using red yarn, work two straight stitches side by side for the mouth, so that they form a flattened V-shape. Colour the cheeks using a red colouring pencil.

DRESS
Make 2 pieces
* Cast on 20 sts in purple.
* 1st row: K.
* Work 3 rows in st st, beg with a K row.
* Next row: K.
* Work 4 rows in st st, beg with a K row.
* Next row: K2, k2tog, K to last 3 sts, ssk, K1. [18 sts]
* Work 3 rows in st st, beg with a P row.
* Rep last 4 rows once more. [16 sts]
* Work 7 rows in st st, beg with a K row.
* K 3 rows.
* Next row: Cast off 2 sts, K2 (3 sts on needle incl st rem from casting off), cast off 6 sts, K to end. [8 sts]

* Work on 5 sts just knitted only, leaving rem 3 sts on needle.
* Next row: Cast off 2 sts, K to end. [3 sts]
* Working on 3 sts just knitted only, K 7 rows.
* Cast off.
* With ws facing, rejoin yarn to 3 sts left on needle.
* K 8 rows.
* Cast off.

MAKING UP
Sew the shoulder and side seams.

SHOES
Make 2
* Using size 2.75 mm (US 2) needles, cast on 8 sts in red.
* 1st row: inc1, K to last 2 sts, inc1, K1. [10 sts]
* Next row: P.
* Rep last 2 rows once more. [12 sts]
* Work 2 rows in st st, beg with a K row.
* Next row: inc1, K to last 2 sts, inc1, K1. [14 sts]
* Next row: P5, cast off 4 sts pwise, P to end. Turn work and cont on these last 5 sts only, leaving rem sts on needle or on a safety pin.
* Work 6 rows in st st, beg with a K row.
* Cast off.
* With rs facing, rejoin yarn to rem 5 sts.
* Work 6 rows in st st, beg with a K row.
* Cast off.

MAKING UP
Fold the shoe pieces in half lengthways with the right side facing inward. Oversew the back and lower seam of the shoes. Turn the right way out. Put the shoes on the doll and secure with a couple of stitches. Work a couple of large straight stitches across the foot to represent the bar of the shoe.

BOW
Make 1
Work an 8-cm (3-in) crochet chain in purple. Arrange it in a figure-of-eight shape with the yarn tails at the centre, and use these yarn tails to sew the bow to the head.

Father Bear

Father Bear is definitely the head of the three bears' household. He has the biggest bed, the biggest chair and, of course, the biggest bowl of porridge. In his red jersey and green trousers with braces, he's a traditional type of bear. But his stern expression and burly build give you the hint that you would be wise not to get on the wrong side of him.

YOU WILL NEED

15 g/½ oz (37 m/40½ yd) pale mustard DK yarn

8 g/¼ oz (20 m/22 yd) red DK yarn

11 g/⅜ oz (27 m/30 yd) green DK yarn

Small amounts of white and black DK yarns

Two small red buttons

10–15 g (⅜–½ oz) polyester toy filling

Green sewing thread

Use size 3 mm (US 2/3) knitting needles.

DOLL

BODY

The body is knitted from the bottom edge upwards and includes the body of the jersey (the jersey sleeves are knitted separately).

Make 2 pieces

✳ Cast on 18 sts in pale mustard.

✳ 1st row: inc1, K to last 2 sts, inc1, K1. [20 sts]

✳ Next row: P.

✳ Next row: K2, m1, K to last 2 sts, m1, K2. [22 sts]

✳ Next row: P.

✳ Rep last 2 rows once more. [24 sts]

✳ Work 8 rows in st st, beg with a K row.

✳ Break pale mustard yarn and join red yarn.

✳ K 2 rows.

✳ Work 6 rows in st st, beg with a K row.

✳ Next row: K2, k2tog, K to last 4 sts, ssk, K2. [22 sts]

✳ Work 3 rows in st st, beg with a P row.

✳ Next row: K2, k2tog, K to last 4 sts, ssk, K2. [20 sts]

✳ Next row: P.

✳ Rep last 2 rows 4 times more. [12 sts]

✳ K 2 rows.

✳ Cast off.

HEAD

The head is knitted from the back of the head to the nose.

Make 2 pieces

* Cast on 14 sts in pale mustard.
* 1st row: inc1, K to last 2 sts, inc1, K1. [16 sts]
* Next row: P.
* Next row: K2, m1, K to last 2 sts, m1, K2. [18 sts]
* Work 11 rows in st st, beg with a P row.
* Next row: K2, k2tog, K2, k2tog, K2, ssk, K2, ssk, K2. [14 sts]
* Next row; P.
* Next row: K2, (k2tog) twice, K2, (ssk) twice, K2. [10 sts]
* Next row: P.
* Next row: K.
* Next row: p2tog, P6, p2tog. [8 sts]
* Next row: k2tog, K4, ssk. [6 sts]
* Cast off kwise.

EARS

Make 2

* Cast on 5 sts in pale mustard.
* Work 2 rows in st st, beg with a K row.
* Next row: k2tog, K1, ssk. [3 sts]
* Next row: P.
* Next row: (K1, m1) twice, K1. [5 sts]
* Work 3 rows in st st, beg with a P row.
* Cast off.

LEGS

The feet and legs are knitted as one piece, starting at the sole of the foot.

Make 2

* Cast on 26 sts in pale mustard.
* Work 5 rows in st st, beg with a K row.
* Next row: P4, cast off 18 sts kwise, P to end. [8 sts]
* Work 8 rows in st st, beg with a K row.
* Cast off.

ARMS

The arms are knitted from the shoulder to the paw.

Make 2

* Cast on 8 sts in pale mustard.
* Work 16 rows in st st, beg with a K row.
* Next row: k2tog, K4, ssk. [6 sts]
* Next row: p2tog, P2, p2tog. [4 sts]
* Cast off.

MAKING UP

With the two head pieces wrong sides together, seam the sides using mattress stitch, leaving the back edge open for stuffing. Stuff the head and close the gap using mattress stitch. With the two body pieces wrong sides together, seam the sides and lower edge using mattress stitch. Stuff the body through the neck edge. Position the head on the neck so that the neck forms a circle on the underside of the head and stitch it in place.

Fold one leg in half lengthways, right sides together, and oversew the top and bottom of the foot. Turn the leg right side out and stitch the back seam, using mattress stitch. Repeat for the second leg. Stuff and sew in place.

Fold one arm in half lengthways, right sides together, and oversew around the paw. Turn the arm right side out and sew the long seam using mattress stitch. Repeat for the second arm. Stuff the arms lightly. Sew the arms in place.

Fold the ear pieces right sides together and oversew around the curved edges. Turn the ears right side out and stitch in place.

Work two French knots in black yarn for the eyes. Work two circles of chain stitch around each eye, using white yarn. Using black yarn, work a small triangle in satin stitch for the nose and add two straight stitches for the mouth.

JERSEY SLEEVES

The main body of the jersey is knitted as part of the bear itself.

Make 2

* Cast on 11 sts in red.
* Work 12 rows in st st, beg with a K row.
* Cast off.

MAKING UP

Sew the side seams of the sleeves using mattress stitch. Oversew the cast-off edges of the sleeves around the top of the arm and roll up the lower edges.

TROUSERS

The trousers are knitted from the bottom edge upwards and is designed to be a loose fit on the bear.

Make 2 pieces

* Cast on 22 sts in green.
* 1st row: inc1, K to last 2 sts, inc1, K1. [24 sts]
* Next row: P.
* Next row: K2, m1, K to last 2 sts, m1, K2. [26 sts]
* Next row: P.
* Rep last 2 rows once more. [28 sts]
* Work 12 rows in st st, beg with a K row.
* K 2 rows.
* Cast off pwise.

TROUSER LEGS

Make 2

* Cast on 14 sts in green.
* K 2 rows.
* Work 3 rows in st st, beg with a P row.
* Cast off.

BRACES

Make 2

* Cast on 34 sts in green.
* 1st row: K.
* Cast off kwise.

MAKING UP

Join the side and lower seams of the trousers using mattress stitch, leaving two gaps along the lower edge that match the position of the legs. Sew the side seams of the trouser legs using mattress stitch. Insert them into the holes on the lower edge of the trousers and oversew them in place. Put the trousers on the bear and sew the braces in place, crossing them at the back. Using green thread, sew the buttons to the front of the braces as shown in the photograph (see page 56).

HOW TO KNIT
Mother Bear

Mother Bear is a gentle-natured creature who puts her family at the heart of everything she does. Dressed sensibly in a comfortable skirt and cardigan, she gets on with everyone and doesn't like to make a fuss. One of her favourite occupations is cooking good, wholesome meals for her family – such as the porridge in this famous story.

YOU WILL NEED

3.5 g/⅛ oz (8.5 m/9½ yd) cream DK yarn

6 g/¼ oz (15 m/16½ yd) pastel pink DK yarn

9 g/⅜ oz (22 m/24 yd) pale mustard DK yarn

6.5 g/¼ oz (16 m/17½ yd) bright pink DK yarn

8 g/¼ oz (20 m/22 yd) aqua DK yarn

Small amounts of white and black DK yarns

One small pink button

One snap fastener

10–15 g (⅜–½ oz) polyester toy filling

White sewing thread

Use size 3 mm (US 2/3) knitting needles.

DOLL

BODY

The body is knitted from the bottom edge upwards and includes the underpants and the shirt.

Make 2 pieces

❊ Cast on 14 sts in cream.

❊ 1st row: inc1, K to last 2 sts, inc1, K1. [16 sts]

❊ Next row: P.

❊ Next row: K2, m1, K to last 2 sts, m1, K2. [18 sts]

❊ Next row: P.

❊ Rep last 2 rows once more. [20 sts]

❊ Work 6 rows in st st, beg with a K row.

❊ Break cream yarn and join pastel pink yarn.

❊ K 2 rows.

❊ Work 6 rows in st st, beg with a K row.

❊ Next row: K2, k2tog, K to last 4 sts, ssk, K2. [18 sts]

❊ Work 3 rows in st st, beg with a P row.

❊ Next row: K2, k2tog, K to last 4 sts, ssk, K2. [16 sts]

❊ Next row: P.

❊ Rep last 2 rows 3 times more. [10 sts]

❊ K 2 rows.

❊ Cast off.

HEAD

The head is knitted from the back of the head to the nose.

Make 2 pieces

* Cast on 12 sts in pale mustard.
* 1st row: inc1, K to last 2 sts, inc1, K1. [14 sts]
* Next row: P.
* Next row: K2, m1, K to last 2 sts, m1, K2. [16 sts]
* Work 9 rows in st st, beg with a P row.
* Next row: K2, (k2tog) twice, K4, (ssk) twice, K2. [12 sts]
* Next row; P.
* Next row: K1, (k2tog) twice, K2, (ssk) twice, K1. [8 sts]
* Next row: P.
* Next row: K.
* Next row: p2tog, P4, p2tog. [6 sts]
* Cast off.

EARS
Make 2
* Cast on 5 sts in pale mustard.
* Work 2 rows in st st, beg with a K row.
* Next row: k2tog, K1, ssk. [3 sts]
* Next row: P.
* Next row: (K1, m1) twice, K1. [5 sts]
* Work 3 rows in st st, beg with a P row.
* Cast off.

LEGS
The feet and legs are knitted as one piece, starting at the sole of the foot.
Make 2
* Cast on 26 sts in pale mustard.
* Work 5 rows in st st, beg with a K row.
* Next row: P4, cast off 18 sts kwise, P to end. [8 sts]
* Work 8 rows in st st, beg with a K row.
* Cast off.

ARMS
The arms are knitted from the shoulder to the paw.
Make 2
* Cast on 8 sts in pastel pink.
* Work 7 rows in st st, beg with a K row.
* Next row: K.
* Break pastel pink yarn and join pale mustard yarn.
* Work 8 rows in st st, beg with a K row.
* Next row: k2tog, K4, ssk. [6 sts]
* Next row: p2tog, P2, p2tog. [4 sts]
* Cast off.

MAKING UP
Sew mother bear together in the same way as father bear, as described on page 57.

Using a single ply of black yarn, work three small straight stitches above each eye to represent the eyelashes.

SKIRT
Make 2 pieces
* Cast on 30 sts in bright pink.
* 1st row: (K2, P2) to last 2 sts, K2.
* Next row: (P2, K2) to last 2 sts, P2.
* Rep these 2 rows 6 times more.
* Next row: (k2tog, p2tog) 7 times, k2tog. [15 sts]
* Cast off kwise.

MAKING UP
Join the side seams of the skirt using mattress stitch.

CARDIGAN
The main body of the cardigan is knitted as one piece.
Make 1
* Cast on 34 sts in aqua.
* K 2 rows.
* Work 10 rows in st st, beg with a K row.
* Next row: K9, turn and work on these 9 sts only, leaving rem sts on needle.
* Next row: P7, K2.
* Next row: K.
* Rep last 2 rows once more.
* Break yarn and rejoin it to rs of rem sts.

* Next row: K16, turn and work on these 16 sts only, leaving rem sts on needle.
* Work 4 rows in st st, beg with a P row.
* Break yarn and rejoin it to rs of rem 9 sts.
* Next row: K.
* Next row: K2, P7.
* Rep last 2 rows once more.
* Next row: K.
* Now work across all 34 sts on needle.
* Next row: K2, P to last 2 sts, K2.
* K 3 rows.
* Cast off.

SLEEVES
Make 2
* Cast on 14 sts in aqua.
* K 2 rows.
* Work 10 rows in st st, beg with a K row.
* Cast off.

MAKING UP
Sew the seams of the sleeves using mattress stitch. Insert them into the armholes of the cardigan and oversew them in place from the inside. Using white thread, sew the button onto the right side of the cardigan. Sew the top of the snap fastener under the button and the bottom of the snap fastener on the corresponding part of the other side of the cardigan.

HOW TO KNIT
Baby Bear

Mother Bear wouldn't want to know this, but her little son is spoilt rotten. Although he looks adorable in his cute blue rompers, Baby Bear is prone to more than the odd tantrum when things don't go his way. He's not prepared to share his toys, his chair or his food with anyone – even a girl as pretty as feisty little Goldilocks.

YOU WILL NEED

10 g/⅜ oz (24 m/26 yd) pale mustard DK yarn

4.5 g/⅛ oz (10.5 m/11½ yd) pale blue DK yarn

5.5 g/¼ oz (13 m/14½ yd) air force blue DK yarn

Small amounts of white and black DK yarns

10–15 g (⅜–½ oz) polyester toy filling

Use size 3 mm (US 2/3) knitting needles.

DOLL

BODY

The body is knitted from the bottom edge upwards and includes the jersey.

Make 2 pieces

❋ Cast on 10 sts in pale mustard.
❋ 1st row: inc1, K to last 2 sts, inc1, K1. [12 sts]
❋ Next row: P.
❋ Next row: K2, m1, K to last 2 sts, m1, K2. [14 sts]
❋ Next row: P.
❋ Rep last 2 rows once more. [16 sts]
❋ Work 4 rows in st st, beg with a K row.
❋ Break pale mustard yarn and join pale blue yarn.
❋ K 2 rows.
❋ Work 4 rows in st st, beg with a K row.
❋ Next row: K2, k2tog, K to last 4 sts, ssk, K2. [14 sts]
❋ Work 3 rows in st st, beg with a P row.
❋ Next row: K2, k2tog, K to last 4 sts, ssk, K2. [12 sts]
❋ Next row: P.
❋ Rep last 2 rows once more. [10 sts]
❋ Work 2 rows in st st, beg with a K row.
❋ K 2 rows.
❋ Cast off.

HEAD

The head is knitted from the back of the head to the nose.

Make 2 pieces

❈ Cast on 12 sts in pale mustard.
❈ 1st row: inc1, K to last 2 sts, inc1, K1. [14 sts]
❈ Next row: P.
❈ Next row: K2, m1, K to last 2 sts, m1, K2. [16 sts]
❈ Work 7 rows in st st, beg with a P row.
❈ Next row: K2, (k2tog) twice, K4, (ssk) twice, K2. [12 sts]
❈ Next row; P.
❈ Next row: K1, (k2tog) twice, K2, (ssk) twice, K1. [8 sts]
❈ Next row: P.
❈ Next row: K.
❈ Next row: p2tog, P4, p2tog. [6 sts]
❈ Cast off.

EARS

Make 2

❈ Cast on 5 sts in pale mustard.
❈ Work 2 rows in st st, beg with a K row.
❈ Next row: k2tog, K1, ssk. [3 sts]
❈ Next row: P.
❈ Next row: (K1, m1) twice, K1. [5 sts]
❈ Work 3 rows in st st, beg with a P row.
❈ Cast off.

LEGS

The feet and legs are knitted in one piece, starting at the sole of the foot.

Make 2

❈ Cast on 22 sts in pale mustard.
❈ Work 5 rows in st st, beg with a K row.
❈ Next row: P4, cast off 14 sts kwise, P to end. [8 sts]
❈ Work 6 rows in st st, beg with a K row.
❈ Cast off.

ARMS

The arms are knitted from the shoulder to the paw.

Make 2

❈ Cast on 7 sts in pale blue.
❈ Work 7 rows in st st, beg with a K row.
❈ Next row: K.
❈ Break pale blue yarn and join pale mustard yarn.
❈ Work 8 rows in st st, beg with a K row.
❈ Next row: k2tog, K3, ssk. [5 sts]
❈ Next row: p2tog, P1, p2tog. [3 sts]
❈ Next row: s1, k2tog, psso. [1 st]
❈ Break yarn and pull it through rem st.

MAKING UP

Sew baby bear together in the same way as father bear, as described on page 57.

ROMPERS

FRONT

Make 1

❈ Cast on 14 sts in air force blue.
❈ 1st row: inc1, K to last 2 sts, inc1, K1. [16 sts]
❈ Next row: P.

❈ Next row: K2, m1, K to last 2 sts, m1, K2. [18 sts]
❈ Next row: P.
❈ Rep last 2 rows once more. [20 sts]
❈ Work 8 rows in st st, beg with a K row.
❈ Next row: P.*
❈ Next row: Cast off 6 sts, K7 (8 sts on needle incl st rem from casting off), cast off 6 sts. [8 sts]
❈ Break yarn and rejoin it to rs of work.
❈ Next row: K.
❈ Next row: K1, P to last st, K1.
❈ Rep these 2 rows once more.
❈ K 3 rows.
❈ Cast off pwise.

BACK

Make 1

❈ work as for front until *.
❈ Cast off kwise.

STRAPS

Make 2

❈ Cast on 20 sts in air force blue.
❈ Cast off.

MAKING UP

Join the side and lower seams of the rompers using mattress stitch, leaving two gaps along the lower edge that match the position of the legs. Put the rompers on the bear and sew the straps in place, crossing them at the back.

The Three Little Pigs

I t happens at some time to every parent. Poor Mother Pig loved her cute triplets, but she just couldn't afford to keep them any longer. The sty wasn't big enough, their appetites had rocketed – and the noise was getting her down. Luckily, all three piglets shared the same upbeat, can-do attitude. Why, they thought, if there wasn't enough room with their mother, they'd simply build a house of their own, put it together with their own little trotters. Better yet, they'd go for a house EACH! Building couldn't be too hard, could it? No sirree!

Piggy No. 1 started first. He drew up a plan and showed it proudly to his brothers: **"Look guys! I'm planning to build my house from straw bales!"** he cried, **"They're light, they're warm, and when I get sick of the view, I can simply tie my home to an outsize balloon and float it to somewhere I prefer!"** He was very, very pleased with his plans. Piggy No. 2 was a little more cautious. **"I think I'll go for sticks to build my house,"** he said. **"I know straw's warm, but it's awfully light – I'm not sure it's tough enough for a house."** Piggy No. 3 had already decided on his building materials. **"I'm using bricks,"** he said firmly. **"I think traditional is sometimes best."** Off they went, all three, to build their houses.

Not far away, there was a forest. And in the forest, as often happens, there lived a Wolf. The Wolf just loved fresh pork, so when he heard there were three little pigs new to the district, he came to call. First, he came to the house of straw. It was certainly handsome, gleaming golden in the sun. The Wolf knocked at the door. **"Little pig, little pig, let me come in!"** Piggy No. 1 was horrified. **"Oh no, not by the hairs of my chinny, chin, chin!"** he squealed. **"Then,"** said the Wolf, **"I'll huff, and I'll puff, and I'll blow your house down!" "Try it!"** said Piggy No. 1 (he was very scared, but he had spirit). So the Wolf huffed and puffed, and the house blew apart. It was only made of straw, after all. And the Wolf had pork for dinner.

Next day, he went to call on Piggy No. 2. Rapping sharply on the door, he called, **"Little pig, little pig, let me come in!"** Piggy No. 2 had his answer ready: **"Oh no, not by the hairs of my chinny, chin, chin!" "Then,"** said the Wolf calmly, **"I'll huff, and I'll puff, and I'll blow your house down!"** The house of wood and twigs was a little stronger than the house of straw, but the Wolf was patient and he blew hard. Eventually, the twig house started to creak and groan – and then suddenly, it blew into little fragments of wood. And the Wolf had pork for dinner again.

His idea had been very successful, so it's hardly surprising that on the third day, the Wolf turned up at the door of the house made of bricks. He lifted the door knocker and let it fall with a thump. **"Little pig, little pig, let me come in!"**

Piggy No. 3 was quick with his answer: **"Oh no, not by the hairs of my chinny, chin, chin!"** "Well, I'll HUFF and I'll PUFF, and I'll BLOW YOUR HOUSE DOWN!" But Piggy No. 3 just laughed. The Wolf was furious. Filling his lungs, he blew an enormous blow. And the house stayed solid. He drew a deeper breath and tried again. No result. Finally, he breathed in deeper than he'd ever breathed before and blew out a great wind of breath. The house stood still. But the Wolf had gone too far: he'd blown so hard that he'd blown himself inside out and he couldn't turn himself back. So that was the end of him.

And what became of Piggy No. 3? Today, he runs a building business, and takes good care of his widowed mother. He always was the brightest of her children.

The Three Little Pigs

Everyone loves a cute piglet, so how much better is it to have three of them? Squishy, pink and vulnerable, this lovable trio are about to take their first steps into the big, wide world. Their flesh is knitted in the palest of pinks and they are all sporting brightly coloured tops and denim-look shorts.

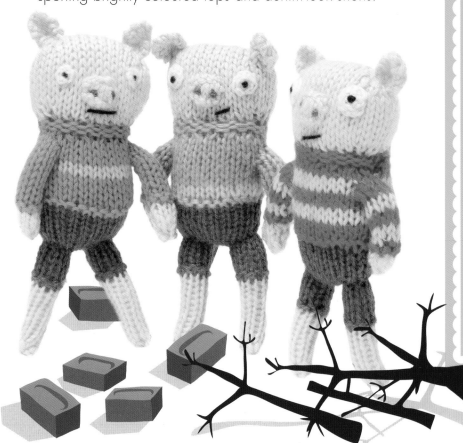

YOU WILL NEED

FOR EACH PIG
6.5 g/¼ oz (16 m/17½ yd) pale pink DK yarn
2.5 g/¹⁄₁₆ oz (6 m/6½ yd) denim blue DK yarn
Very small amounts of white, black and mauve DK yarns
10–15 g (⅜–½ oz) polyester toy filling

FOR PIG WITH RED JUMPER
2 g/¹⁄₁₆ oz (5 m/5½ yd) red DK yarn
1.5 g/¹⁄₁₆ oz (3 m/3½ yd) cream DK yarn

FOR PIG WITH TURQUOISE JUMPER
3 g/⅛ oz (6.5 m/7 yd) turquoise DK yarn
1 g/¹⁄₁₆ oz (1.5 m/2 yd) cream DK yarn

FOR PIG WITH OLIVE GREEN JUMPER
3 g/⅛ oz (6.5 m/7 yd) olive green DK yarn
1 g/¹⁄₁₆ oz (1.5 m/2 yd) cream DK yarn

Use size 3 mm (US 2/3) knitting needles, except when instructed to use size 2.75 mm (US 2) knitting needles.

DOLL

BODY & HEAD
The body and head are knitted together from the base of the body upwards and include the shorts and T-shirt.
Make 2 pieces
❋ Cast on 12 sts in denim blue.
❋ Work 8 rows in st st, beg with a K row.

For pig with red jumper
❋ Break yarn and join red yarn.
❋ K 2 rows.
❋ Next row: K2, m1, K1, m1, K to last 3 sts, m1, K1, m1, K2. [16 sts]
❋ Next row: P.

❋ Leave red yarn at side of work and join cream yarn.
❋ Work 2 rows in st st, beg with a K row.
❋ Leave cream yarn at side of work and join red yarn.
❋ Work 2 rows in st st, beg with a K row.
❋ Rep last 4 rows once more.
❋ Break cream yarn.
❋ Next row: K2, (k2tog) 3 times, (ssk) 3 times, K2. [10 sts]
❋ Next row: K.
❋ Next row: P.
❋ Break red yarn and join pale pink yarn.
❋ * Next row: P.
❋ Next row: K2, (m1, K1) 3 times, (K1, m1) 3 times, K2. [16 sts]

❋ Next row: P.
❋ Next row: K2, m1, K1, m1, K to last 3 sts, m1, K1, m1, K2. [20 sts]
❋ Work 7 rows in st st, beg with a P row.
❋ Next row: K2, (k2tog) twice, K to last 6 sts, (ssk) twice, K2. [16 sts]
❋ Next row: p2tog, P to last 2 sts, p2tog. [14 sts]
❋ Next row: (k2tog) twice, K to last 4 sts, (ssk) twice. [10 sts]
❋ Cast off kwise.

For pig with turquoise jumper
❋ Break yarn and join turquoise yarn.
❋ K 2 rows.

❊ Next row: K2, m1, K1, m1, K to last
3 sts, m1, K1, m1, K2. [16 sts]
❊ Work 3 rows in st st, beg with a P row.
❊ Leave turquoise yarn at side of work
and join cream yarn.
❊ Work 2 rows in st st, beg with a K row.
❊ Break cream yarn and rejoin
turquoise yarn.
❊ Work 4 rows in st st, beg with a K row.
❊ Next row: K2, (k2tog) 3 times, (ssk)
3 times, K2. [10 sts]
❊ Next row: K.
❊ Next row: P.
❊ Break turquoise yarn and join pale
pink yarn.
❊ Continue as for pig with red jumper
from *.

For pig with olive green jumper
❊ Break yarn and join olive green yarn.
❊ K 2 rows.
❊ Leave olive green yarn at side of work
and join cream yarn.
❊ Next row: K2, m1, K1, m1, K to last
3 sts, m1, K1, m1, K2. [16 sts]
❊ Next row: P.
❊ Break cream yarn and rejoin olive
green yarn.
❊ Work 8 rows in st st, beg with a K row.
❊ Next row: K2, (k2tog) 3 times,
(ssk) 3 times, K2. [10 sts]
❊ Next row: K.
❊ Next row: P.
❊ Break olive green yarn and join pale
pink yarn.
❊ Continue as for pig with red jumper
from *.

LEGS
The legs are knitted from the top edge
downwards.
Make 2
❊ Cast on 10 sts in denim blue.
❊ Work 5 rows in st st, beg with a K row.
❊ Next row: K.
❊ Break yarn and join pale pink yarn.
❊ Next row: k2tog, K to last 2 sts, ssk.
[8 sts]
❊ Work 11 rows in st st, beg with a P row.
❊ Next row: (k2tog) twice, (ssk) twice. [4 sts]
❊ Break yarn and thread it through rem
sts. Pull up quite tightly and secure.

ARMS
The arms are knitted from the top edge
downwards.
Make 2

For pig with red jumper
❊ Cast on 8 sts in red.
❊ Work 2 rows in st st, beg with a K row.
❊ Leave red yarn at side of work and join
cream yarn.
❊ Work 2 rows in st st, beg with a K row.
❊ Leave cream yarn at side of work and
join red yarn.
❊ Work 2 rows in st st, beg with a K row.
❊ Leave red yarn at side of work and join
cream yarn.
❊ Work 2 rows in st st, beg with a K row.
Break cream yarn.
❊ K 2 rows in red yarn. Break red yarn
and join pale pink yarn.
❊ Work 4 rows in st st, beg with a K row.
❊ Next row: (k2tog) twice, (ssk) twice.
[4 sts]
❊ Thread yarn through rem sts. Pull up
quite tightly and secure.

For pig with turquoise jumper
❊ Cast on 8 sts in turquoise.
❊ Work 8 rows in st st, beg with a K row.
❊ K 2 rows.
❊ Break turquoise yarn and join pale
pink yarn.
❊ Work 4 rows in st st, beg with a K row.
❊ Next row: (k2tog) twice, (ssk) twice.
[4 sts]
❊ Thread yarn through rem sts. Pull up
quite tightly and secure.

For pig with olive green jumper
❊ Cast on 8 sts in olive green.
❊ Work 8 rows in st st, beg with a K row.
❊ K 2 rows.
❊ Break olive green yarn and join pale
pink yarn.
❊ Work 4 rows in st st, beg with a K row.
❊ Next row: (k2tog) twice, (ssk) twice.
[4 sts]
❊ Thread yarn through rem sts. Pull up
quite tightly and secure.

EARS
Make 2
❊ Using size 2.75 mm (US 2) needles,
cast on 4 sts in pale pink.
❊ 1st row: inc1, K1, inc1, K1. [6 sts]
❊ K 3 rows.
❊ Next row: k2tog, K2, ssk. [4 sts]
❊ Next row: K.
❊ Next row: k2tog, ssk. [2 sts]
❊ Next row: K.
❊ Next row: k2tog. Break yarn and pull it
through rem st.

SNOUT
Make 1
❊ Using size 2.75 mm (US 2) needles,
cast on 4 sts in pale pink.
❊ 1st row: inc1, K1, inc1, K1. [6 sts]
❊ Next row: P.
❊ Next row: k2tog, K2, ssk. [4 sts]
❊ Cast off kwise.

MAKING UP
With the two head and body pieces right
sides together, oversew around the head.
Turn the piece right side out and sew
the side seams in matching yarns, using
mattress stitch and leaving the lower edge
open for stuffing. Stuff the pig and sew
the gap closed.

Fold the arm and leg pieces right
sides together and oversew around the
hands and feet. Turn the pieces the right
side out and sew the long seams, using
mattress stitch.

Stuff the arms and legs and sew
in place.

Sew the ears in place, curving the
lower edge slightly.

Oversew the snout in place.

Work two French knots for
the eyes using black yarn.
Work two circles of chain
stitch around each eye,
using white yarn.

On the snout, work
two French knots for the
nostrils using mauve yarn.

Work a straight
stitch for the mouth,
using a divided strand
of black yarn.

Beauty & the Beast

Beauty was rightly named. She was pretty and she was kind. And her sisters (she had two) were so ugly, greedy and mean that she looked even better next to them. She was her father's favourite, too. When the merchant asked his girls what he should bring them from a trip into town, the older two demanded fine dresses and jewels. Little Beauty only wanted a red rose. Halfway home, Beauty's father realized that he'd forgotten her simple gift, but he was passing a grand house with a whole hedge of roses, so he picked one for her. Immediately there was a great roar, and a hideous Beast rushed up and called him a thief. Trembling, the merchant explained that he wanted the rose for his youngest daughter. And the Beast gave him a horrible choice: he could be killed at once, or he could fetch Beauty back to live with the Beast and keep him company.

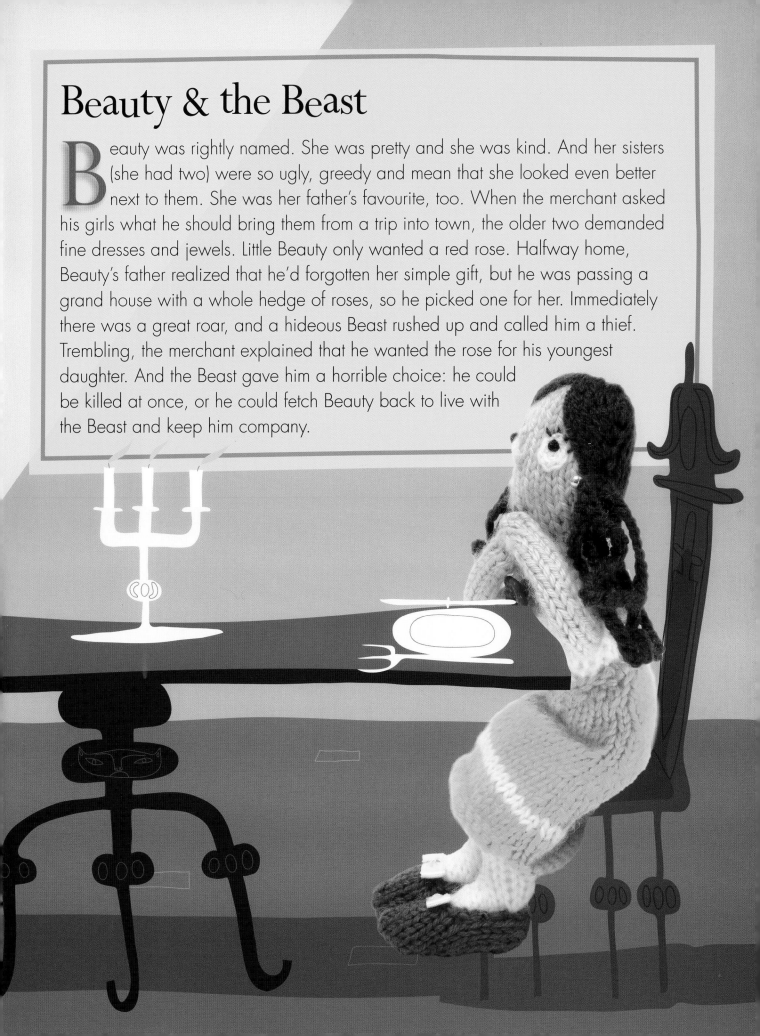

The merchant was sad and didn't know what to do. He returned home, but decided he should go back and die instead of sending Beauty into the Beast's clutches. He said goodbye to his daughters. The elder two were too busy trying on their new finery to pay much attention. Beauty, however, listened to the story and talked her father into letting her go in his stead. **"I expect the Beast's just lonely,"** she said gently. **"Perhaps I can change his ways."** Even Beauty trembled, though, when she first set sight on the Beast's horrible features. She told herself firmly that handsome is as handsome does, and kept busy cooking him nutritious meals and tidying up the gloomy great house. Over the months that followed, she even became rather fond of him.

On one thing she stood firm: every week he asked her to marry him. And every week she refused and had to sit calmly while he ranted and raved about her ingratitude. A whole year passed and Beauty was desperate to visit her family. Very reluctantly, the Beast gave her permission, but made her promise she'd stay away only a month. She agreed, but when she reached home she was so delighted to see her friends again that she forgot her promise. The month ended, another passed, and she still hadn't thought about going back.

One day, Beauty was arranging her hair and when she looked in the mirror, instead of her own lovely face, she saw instead a reflection of the Beast, lying ill in his rose garden. Beauty was horrified. Pausing only to say goodbye to her father, she set off back to the mansion straight away. She found the Beast in the garden, barely conscious and terribly thin. Crying at the sight of him, she helped him up, hugging and kissing him tenderly. **"I've been selfish and thoughtless,"** she sobbed. **"Dear Beast, if you still want me to, I'll marry you!"** And as the words left her lips, something happened: all of a sudden, the Beast transformed into a young man, tall, handsome and smiling.

He explained to the astounded Beauty that he had been placed under an enchantment by a wicked fairy, who had decreed that he would remain a Beast until a lovely girl agreed to have him as a husband. So Beauty married the prince and everyone was thrilled for them. Except the ugly sisters, of course – they were positively eaten up with jealousy.

HOW TO KNIT

Beauty

Beautiful, kind, plucky and intelligent – Beauty was almost perfect. But like any girl, she had dreams of marrying a handsome prince. An ugly monster was not going to make the grade, even if he did happen to be rich and good hearted. She is dressed here in a classic-style dress in shades of deep gold and pale yellow that beautifully complement her long, dark brown tresses.

YOU WILL NEED

6 g/¼ oz (14 m/15½ yd) beige DK yarn

2 g/¹⁄₁₆ oz (5 m/5½ yd) dark brown DK yarn

5 g/¼ oz (11.5 m/13 yd) pale yellow DK yarn

8 g/¼ oz (19 m/21 yd) deep yellow DK yarn

2 g/¹⁄₁₆ oz (5 m/5½ yd) dark pink DK yarn

Small amounts of black and white DK yarns

A very small amount of dark red DK yarn

One medium dark pink flower shaped button

Two tiny readymade bows in pale yellow

Two 4-mm/⅛-in gold beads

Gold sewing thread

10–15 g (⅜–½ oz) polyester toy filling

Pink colouring pencil

Use size 3 mm (US 2/3) knitting needles, except when instructed to use size 2.75 mm (US 2) knitting needles, and a size 3.25 mm (US D-3) crochet hook

DOLL

HEAD
The head is knitted from the base of the chin to the top of the forehead.

Front
Make 1
❋ Cast on 6 sts in beige.
❋ 1st row: K1, inc1, K2, inc1, K1. [8 sts]
❋ Next row: P.
❋ Next row: K1, m1, K to last st, m1, K1. [10 sts]
❋ Next row: P.
❋ Rep last 2 rows twice more.* [14 sts]
❋ Work 10 rows in st st, beg with a K row.
❋ Next row: K2, k2tog, K6, ssk, K2. [12 sts]
❋ Next row: p2tog, P8, p2tog. [10 sts]
❋ Cast off.

Back
Make 1
❋ Work as for front to *.
❋ Break beige yarn and join dark brown yarn.

* Work 10 rows in st st, beg with a K row.
* Next row: K2, k2tog, K6, ssk, K2. [12 sts]
* Next row: p2tog, P8, p2tog. [10 sts]
* Cast off.

BODY
The body is knitted from the lower edge to the neck edge.
Make 2 pieces
* Cast on 14 sts in pale yellow.
* Work 6 rows in st st, beg with a K row.
* Next row: K2, (k2tog) twice, K2, (ssk) twice, K2. [10 sts]
* Next row: P.
* Next row: K2, k2tog, K2, ssk, K2. [8 sts]
* Next row: P.
* Next row: K2, m1, K to last 2 sts, m1, K2. [10 sts]
* Next row: P.
* Rep last 2 rows once more. [12 sts]
* Work 3 rows in st st, beg with a K row.
* Next row: K.
* Break pale yellow yarn and join beige yarn.
* Work 2 rows in st st, beg with a K row.
* Next row; Cast off 1 st, K to end. [11 sts]
* Next row: Cast off 1 st pwise, P to end. [10 sts]
* Cast off.

LEGS
The feet and legs are knitted as one piece, starting at the sole of the foot.
Make 2
* Cast on 24 sts in white.
* Work 4 rows in st st, beg with a K row.
* Next row: K5, cast off 14 sts, K5. [10 sts]
* Work 21 rows in st st, beg with a P row.
* Cast off.

ARMS
The arms are knitted from the top of the shoulder to the tip of the hand.
Make 2
* Cast on 9 sts in beige.
* Work 22 rows in st st, beg with a K row.

* Next row: K2, k2tog, K1, ssk, K2. [7 sts]
* Next row: p2tog, P3, p2tog. [5 sts]
* Next row: k2tog, K1, ssk. [3 sts]
* Break yarn and thread through rem sts.

HAIR
* Work six 13-cm (5¼-in) crochet chains in dark brown yarn.

MAKING UP
Place the two head pieces right sides together and oversew around the edges, leaving the top of the head open for turning and stuffing. Turn the head right side out, stuff and close the gap using mattress stitch. Sew the body together using mattress stitch, leaving the lower edge open for turning and stuffing. Stuff and close the gap. Sew the head to the body.

Fold one leg in half lengthways, right sides together, and oversew the top and lower edge of the foot. Turn the leg right side out and sew the back seam using mattress stitch. Repeat for the second leg. Stuff the legs and feet.

Fold one arm in half lengthways, right sides together, and oversew around the hand. Turn the arm right side out and sew the long seam using mattress stitch. Repeat for the second arm. The arms do not need stuffing.

Sew the arms and legs in place.

Form each crochet chain into a loop and join three loops to each side of the head using the yarn tails.

Work two French knots in black yarn for the eyes. Work two circles of chain stitch around each eye, using white yarn. Using a separated strand of black yarn, work four straight stitches above each eye to represent the eyelashes. Work two short rows of chain stitch in flesh yarn for the nose.

Divide a short length of dark red yarn into two thinner strands. Work two straight stitches to form a V-shape for the mouth, then work another set or two of stitches over these stitches to make the mouth fuller.

Using gold thread, sew the two gold beads in position for the earrings. Colour the cheeks, using a pink colouring pencil.

SKIRT OF DRESS

Back
Make 1
* Cast on 24 sts in deep yellow.
* K 2 rows.
* Work 3 rows in st st, beg with a P row.
* Leave deep yellow yarn at the side and join pale yellow yarn.
* Work 2 rows in st st, beg with a K row.
* Break pale yellow yarn and use deep yellow yarn.
* Work 2 rows in st st, beg with a K row.*
* Next row: K2, k2tog, K to last 4 sts, ssk, K2. [22 sts]
* Work 3 rows in st st, beg with a P row.
* Rep last 4 rows 3 times more. [16 sts]
* Next row: K2, k2tog, K to last 4 sts, ssk, K2. [14 sts]
* Next row: P.
* Cast off pwise.

Front
Make 1
* Work as for back to *.
* Next row: K2, k2tog, K to last 4 sts, ssk, K2. [22 sts]
* Work 3 rows in st st, beg with a P row.
* Rep last 4 rows twice more. [18 sts]
* Next row: K2, k2tog, K5. Turn and work on these 8 sts only.
* Next row: p2tog, P6. [7 sts]
* Next row: K5, ssk. [6 sts]
* Next row: p2tog, P4. [5 sts]
* Next row: K1, k2tog, ssk. [3 sts]
* Next row: p2tog, P1. [2 sts]
* Next row: k2tog. Break yarn and pull it through rem st.
* With rs facing, rejoin yarn to rem 9 sts.
* Next row: K5, ssk, K2. [8 sts]
* Next row: P6, p2tog. [7 sts]
* Next row: k2tog, K5. [6 sts]
* Next row: P4, p2tog. [5 sts]
* Next row: k2tog, ssk, K1. [3 sts]
* Next row: P1, p2tog. [2 sts]
* Next row: k2tog. Break yarn and pull it through rem st.

COLLAR
Make 1
❋ Cast on 32 sts in deep yellow.
❋ Work 3 rows in st st, beg with a K row.
❋ Cast off kwise.

MAKING UP
Join the side seams of the skirt using mattress stitch. Oversew the back waist of the skirt around the doll's waist and oversew the V shape in place at the front. Using deep yellow yarn, work a row of chain stitch at the front of the dress where the skirt meets the body. Position the collar so that the row edges are at the front and the cast-off edge is at the top. Stitch in place at the front and back. Using gold thread, stitch the dark pink button in position.

SHOES
Make 2
❋ Using size 2.75 mm (US 2) needles, cast on 8 sts in dark pink.
❋ 1st row: inc1, K to last 2 sts, inc1, K1. [10 sts]
❋ Next row: P.
❋ Rep last 2 rows once more. [12 sts]
❋ Work 2 rows in st st, beg with a K row.
❋ Next row: inc1, K to last 2 sts, inc1, K1. [14 sts]
❋ Next row: P5, cast off 4 sts pwise, P to end. Turn work and cont on these last 5 sts only, leaving rem sts on needle or on a safety pin.
❋ Work 6 rows in st st, beg with a K row.
❋ Cast off.
❋ With rs facing, rejoin yarn to rem sts.
❋ Work 6 rows in st st, beg with a K row.
❋ Cast off.

MAKING UP
Fold the shoe pieces in half lengthways with the right side facing inward. Oversew the back and lower seam of the shoes. Turn the right way out. Put the shoes on the doll and secure with a couple of stitches. Using gold sewing thread, stitch the two small bows to the front of the shoes.

HOW TO KNIT
The Beast

Everyone knows that real beauty is on the inside and that it shouldn't matter what a person looks like – but sometimes there are limits. The Beast is an ugly brute, but inside him there is a lovely person struggling to get out! Dressed in casually elegant royal blue and navy, with just a touch of gold to demonstrate his fine status, the Beast does his best to detract from his lack of good looks.

YOU WILL NEED

FOR THE PRINCE

6.5 g/¼ oz (16 m/17½ yd) flesh DK yarn

1.5 g/¹⁄₁₆ oz (3 m/3½ yd) rust DK yarn

5 g/¼ oz (12 m/13 yd) white DK yarn

4 g/⅛ oz (9.5 m/10½ yd) dark olive DK yarn

9 g/⅜ oz (22 m/24 yd) royal blue DK yarn

8 g/¼ oz (19 m/21 yd) navy blue DK yarn

Very small amounts of black and mid-pink
DK yarns

Four 5-mm round gold sequins

Four 3-mm gold beads

Two 7-mm square gold sequins

Gold sewing thread

10–15 g (⅜–½ oz) polyester toy filling

Red colouring pencil

FOR THE BEAST MASK & PAWS

4.5 g/⅛ oz (11 m/12 yd) camel DK yarn

Small amounts of pale green, ochre and white
DK yarns

Small amount of chunky soft beige yarn

Very small amounts of red and black DK yarns

Use size 3 mm (US 2/3) knitting
needles, except when instructed to use
size 2.75 mm (US 2) knitting needles.

DOLL

HEAD

Front
Make 1
❋ Cast on 12 sts in flesh.
❋ 1st row: K1, inc1, K to last 3 sts, inc1,
  K2.* [14 sts]
❋ Work 15 rows in st st, beg with a
  P row.
❋ Next row: K2, k2tog, K to last 4 sts,
  ssk, K2. [12 sts]
❋ Next row: p2tog, P to last 2 sts, p2tog.
  [10 sts]
❋ Rep last 2 rows once more. [6 sts]
❋ Cast off.

Back
Make 1
❋ Work as for front to *.
❋ Work 11 rows in st st, beg with a
  P row.
❋ Break yarn and join rust yarn.
❋ Work 4 rows in st st, beg with a K row.
❋ Next row: K2, k2tog, K to last 4 sts,
  ssk, K2. [12 sts]
❋ Next row: p2tog, P to last 2 sts, p2tog.
  [10 sts]
❋ Rep last 2 rows once more. [6 sts]
❋ Cast off.

EARS
Make 2
❋ Using size 2.75 mm (US 2) needles,
  cast on 4 sts in flesh.
❋ 1st row: (k2tog) twice. [2 sts]
❋ Next row: p2tog.
❋ Break yarn and pull it through rem st.

BODY
Make 2 pieces
❋ Cast on 14 sts in white.
❋ Work 20 rows in st st, beg with a
  K row.
❋ Next row: Cast off 1 st, K to end.
  [13 sts]
❋ Next row: Cast off 1 st pwise,
  P to end. [12 sts]
❋ Cast off.

LEGS

The boots and legs are knitted as one piece, starting at the sole of the boot.
Make 2

✳ Cast on 28 sts in dark olive.
✳ Work 4 rows in st st, beg with a K row.
✳ Next row: K6, cast off 16 sts, K to end. [12 sts]
✳ Work 10 rows in st st, beg with a P row.
✳ Next row: K.
✳ Break dark olive yarn and join flesh yarn.
✳ Work 14 rows in st st, beg with a K row.
✳ Cast off.

ARMS

The arms are knitted from the top of the shoulder to the tip of the hand.
Make 2

✳ Cast on 10 sts in royal blue.
✳ Work 18 rows in st st, beg with a K row.
✳ Break royal blue yarn and join white yarn.
✳ K 4 rows.
✳ Break white yarn and join flesh yarn.
✳ Work 2 rows in st st, beg with a K row.
✳ Next row: K2, k2tog, K2, ssk, K2. [8 sts]
✳ Next row: p2tog, P4, p2tog. [6 sts]
✳ Cast off.

MAKING UP

Place the two head pieces right sides together and oversew around the edges, leaving the top of the head open for turning and stuffing. Turn the head right side out, stuff and close the gap using mattress stitch. Sew the ears in place. Sew the body together using mattress stitch, leaving the lower edge open for turning and stuffing. Stuff and close the gap. Sew the head to the body.

Fold one leg in half lengthways, right sides together, and oversew the top and lower edge of the boot. Turn the leg right side out and sew the back seam using mattress stitch. Repeat for the second leg. Stuff the legs and boots.

Fold one arm in half lengthways, right sides together, and oversew around the hand. Turn the arm right side out and sew the long seam using mattress stitch. Repeat for the second arm. The arms do not need stuffing.

Sew the arms and legs in place. Using gold thread, sew a square sequin to the top of each boot.

Using rust yarn, work a few rows of chain stitch at the front of the head for the hair as shown in the photograph (see page 75).

Work two French knots in black yarn for the eyes. Work two circles of chain stitch around each eye, using white yarn. Work two short rows of chain stitch in flesh yarn for the nose.

Using mid-pink yarn, work two straight stitches side by side for the mouth, so that they form a flattened V-shape. Colour the cheeks using a red colouring pencil.

JACKET

The two front sides and the back of the jacket are knitted as one piece, from the lower edge to the neck edge. The sleeves have been knitted as part of the doll.
Make 1

✳ Cast on 10 sts in royal blue.
✳ 1st row: K1, inc1, K6, inc1, K1. [12 sts]
✳ Next row: K1, P to last st, K1.
✳ Next row: K1, m1, K to last st, m1, K1. [14 sts]
✳ Next row: K1, P to last st, K1.
✳ Rep last 2 rows twice times more. [18 sts]
✳ Next row: K.
✳ Next row: K1, P to last st, K1
✳ Rep last 2 rows 4 times more.
✳ Next row: Cast on 9 sts, K to end. [27 sts]

✳ Next row: Cast on 9 sts, K9, P18, K to end. [36 sts]
✳ Next row: K.
✳ Next row: K2, P to last 2 sts, K2.
✳ Rep last 2 rows 4 times more.
✳ Next row: K11, turn and work on these sts only, leaving rem sts on needle.
✳ Next row: P9, K2.
✳ Next row: K.
✳ Next row: P9, K2.
✳ Rep last 2 rows once more.
✳ Next row: K.
✳ Break yarn and leave sts on needle.
✳ With rs facing, join yarn to rem sts.
✳ Next row: K14.
✳ Turn and work on these sts only.
✳ Work 6 rows in st st, beg with a P row.
✳ Break yarn and leave sts on needle.
✳ With rs facing, join yarn to rem 11 sts on left-hand needle.
✳ Next row: K.
✳ Next row: K2, P9.
✳ Next row: K.
✳ Rep last 2 rows twice more.
✳ Now work across all 36 sts on needle.
✳ Next row: Cast off 5 sts kwise, P7 [8 sts on needle, including rem st from casting off], (p2tog) twice, P2, (p2tog) twice, P to end. [27 sts]
✳ Next row: Cast off 5 sts, K to end. [22 sts]
✳ K 2 rows.
✳ Cast off.

MAKING UP

Put the jacket on the doll and oversew the armhole edges around the top of the arms. Overlap the jacket fronts and sew the four sequins and beads in place for the buttons.

TROUSERS

The trousers are knitted as one piece.
Make 1

✳ Cast on 14 sts for first leg in navy.
✳ K 2 rows.
✳ Work 23 rows in st st, beg with a P row.
✳ Break yarn and leave sts on spare needle.
✳ Work a second trouser leg exactly as the first, but don't break yarn.

❋ Next row: K14 sts from second trouser leg, then knit across 14 sts from first trouser leg. [28 sts]
❋ Work 9 rows in st st, beg with a P row.
❋ Next row: (K1, P1) to end.
❋ Rep last row once more.
❋ Cast off quite loosely, keeping to the K1, P1 pattern.

MAKING UP
Using mattress stitch, join the back seam so that the lowest part of the seam is level with the crotch. Then join the two inside leg seams, again using mattress stitch.

MASK
Make 2 pieces
❋ Cast on 22 sts in camel.
❋ K 2 rows.
❋ Next row: P.
❋ Next row: K2, k2tog, K to last 4 sts, ssk, K2. [20 sts]
❋ Next row: P.
❋ Rep last 2 rows twice more. [16 sts]
❋ Work 14 rows in st st, beg with a K row.
❋ Next row: K2, k2tog, K1, k2tog, K2, ssk, K1, ssk, K2. [12 sts]
❋ Next row: P.
❋ Next row: K2, (k2tog) twice, (ssk) twice, K2. [8 sts]
❋ Cast off kwise.

HORNS
Make 2
❋ Cast on 2 sts in white.
❋ K 1 row.
❋ Cast off.

MAKING UP
Join the side and top seams of the mask using mattress stitch. Using black yarn, work two French knots for the eyes. Using pale green yarn, work two circles of chain stitch around each eye. Using black yarn, work a triangle of satin stitch for the nose. Work a row of chain stitch at each side of the nose, using ochre yarn. Work two French knots for the nostrils, using white yarn. Work a row of back stitch for the mouth, using red yarn. Work a couple of straight stitches in white yarn for the teeth.

Oversew the side seams of the horns and stitch them in place.
Cut several lengths of ochre and chunky beige yarn. Sew one small bunch to the top of the head and the other to the chin.

MITTS
Make 2
❋ Cast on 12 sts in camel.
❋ K 2 rows.
❋ Next row: P.
❋ Work 4 rows in st st, beg with a K row.
❋ Next row: K1, k2tog, K1, k2tog, ssk, K1, ssk, K1. [8 sts]
❋ Next row: p2tog, P4, p2tog. [6 sts]
❋ Break yarn, thread it through rem sts and secure.

MAKING UP
Seam the mitts together using mattress stitch. Using black yarn, work three French knots at the end of each mitt to represent the claws.

The Sisters

The world of these selfish sisters seems to be one of constant bad hair days and wardrobe malfunctions. They just couldn't be more different from their lovely sister, Beauty. The two sisters are knitted identically – the only difference is the colours of the clothes and the colour and type of yarn used for the hair. The colours for the second sister are given in brackets.

YOU WILL NEED

FOR EACH SISTER
8 g/¼ oz (20 m/22 yd) flesh DK yarn
14 g/½ oz (32 m/35 yd) white DK yarn
5 g/¼ oz (11.5 m/13 yd) soft turquoise (orange) DK yarn
14.5 g/½ oz (35 m/38 yd) purple (lime green) DK yarn
2.5 g/¹⁄₁₆ oz (5.5 m/6 yd) red (bright turquoise) DK yarn
3.5 g/⅛ oz (8 m/9 yd) ochre mohair (rust DK) yarn
Very small amounts of black and red DK yarns
Sewing thread
20–25 g (¾–⅞ oz) polyester toy filling

FOR THE BLONDE SISTER, YOU WILL ALSO NEED
An elasticated cream bead bracelet
Two pearl buttons
Two brass rings
A readymade pink ribbon rose

FOR THE RED-HAIRED SISTER, YOU WILL ALSO NEED
An elasticated green bead bracelet
Two crystal-style buttons
Two small pearl beads
A readymade fabric flower

Use size 3 mm (US 2/3) knitting needles, except when instructed to use size 2.75 mm (US 2) knitting needles.

DOLL

HEAD
The head pieces are knitted from the forehead down to the chin.
Make 2 pieces
❋ Cast on 14 sts in flesh.
❋ Work 12 rows in st st, beg with a K row.
❋ Next row: K1, m1, K12, m1, K1. [16 sts]
❋ Work 7 rows in st st, beg with a P row.
❋ Cast off.

BODY

The body is knitted from the lower edge to the neck edge and includes the underpants and the bodice of the dress.
Make 2 pieces
✲ Cast on 18 sts in white.
✲ Work 4 rows in st st, beg with a K row.
✲ Break white yarn and join soft turquoise (orange) yarn.
✲ Work 17 rows in st st, beg with a K row.
✲ Next row: K.
✲ Break soft turquoise (orange) yarn and join flesh yarn.
✲ Work 2 rows in st st, beg with a K row.
✲ Next row: Cast off 1 st, K to end. [17 sts]
✲ Next row: Cast off 1 st pwise, P to end. [16 sts]
✲ Cast off.

LEGS

The feet and legs are knitted as one piece, starting at the sole of the foot.
Make 2
✲ Cast on 28 sts in white.
✲ Work 4 rows in st st, beg with a K row.
✲ Next row: K7, cast off 14 sts, K to end. [14 sts]
✲ Work 21 rows in st st, beg with a P row.
✲ Cast off.

ARMS

The arms are knitted from the top of the shoulder to the tip of the hand.
Make 2
✲ Cast on 9 sts in soft turquoise (orange).
✲ Work 2 rows in st st, beg with a K row.
✲ Next row: (K1, m1) to last st, K1. [17 sts]
✲ Work 5 rows in st st, beg with a P row.
✲ Next row: K1, (k2tog) 8 times. [9 sts]
✲ Next row: K.
✲ Break soft turquoise (orange) yarn and join flesh yarn.
✲ Work 13 rows in st st, beg with a K row.
✲ Next row: p2tog, P5, p2tog. [7 sts]
✲ Next row: K1, k2tog, K1, ssk, K1. [5 sts]
✲ Next row: p2tog, P1, p2tog. [3 sts]
✲ Next row: s1, k2tog, psso. [1 st]
✲ Break yarn and pull it through rem st.

MAKING UP

Place the two head pieces right sides together and oversew around the edges, leaving the top of the head open for turning and stuffing. Turn the head right side out, stuff and close the gap using mattress stitch. Sew the body together using mattress stitch, leaving the lower edge open for turning and stuffing. Stuff and close the gap. Sew the head to the body.

Fold one leg in half lengthways, right sides together, and oversew the top and lower edge of the feet. Turn the leg right side out and sew the back seam using mattress stitch. Repeat for the second leg. Stuff the legs and feet.

Fold one arm in half lengthways, right sides together, and oversew around the hand. Turn the arm right side out and sew the long seam using mattress stitch. Repeat for the second arm. Stuff the sleeve part of the arms.

Sew the arms and legs in place.

Cut the yarn for the hair into 70-cm (27.5-in) lengths and gather together in a bunch. Secure the centre of the lengths to the top of the head and at each side of the face. Then take the yarn bunches at the sides back to the top of the head and secure again. Plait the ends of the yarn, twist the hair into a bun and secure.

Work two French knots in black yarn for the eyes. Work a circle of chain stitch around each eye, using white yarn. Using a separated strand of black yarn, work four straight stitches above each eye to represent the eyelashes. Using flesh yarn, work two short rows of chain stitch for the nose. To make the nose more prominent, work two more rows of chain stitch on these rows.

Divide a short length of red yarn into two thinner strands. Work two straight stitches to form a V-shape for the mouth, then work another two straight stitches over these stitches to make the mouth fuller.

Sew the pearl beads or brass rings in position for the earrings, using flesh yarn. Sew or stick the flowers in the hair.

Colour the cheeks using a red colouring pencil.

SKIRT OF DRESS
Make 2 pieces
✲ Cast on 30 sts in purple (lime green).
✲ K 2 rows.
✲ Work 4 rows in st st, beg with a P row.
✲ Next row: K.
✲ Next row: K1, (yf, k2tog) to last st, K1.
✲ Next row: K.
✲ Work 14 rows in st st, beg with a K row.
✲ Next row: K2, k2tog, K to last 4 sts, ssk, K2. [28 sts]
✲ Next row: P.
✲ Rep last 2 rows 4 times more. [20 sts]
✲ Cast off pwise.

MAKING UP

Join the side seams of the skirt using mattress stitch. Oversew the waist of the skirt in place. Sew the buttons in position.

SHOES
Make 2
✲ Using size 2.75 mm (US 2) needles, cast on 8 sts in red (bright turquoise).
✲ 1st row: inc1, K to last 2 sts, inc1, K1. [10 sts]
✲ Next row: P.
✲ Rep last 2 rows once more. [12 sts]
✲ Work 2 rows in st st, beg with a K row.
✲ Next row: inc1, K to last 2 sts, inc1, K1. [14 sts]
✲ Next row: P5, cast off 4 sts pwise, P to end. Turn work and cont on these last 5 sts only, leaving rem sts on needle or on a safety pin.
✲ Work 8 rows in st st, beg with a K row.
✲ Cast off.
✲ With rs facing, rejoin yarn to rem 5 sts.
✲ Work 8 rows in st st, beg with a K row.
✲ Cast off.

MAKING UP

Fold the shoe pieces in half lengthways with the right side facing inward. Oversew the back and lower seam of the shoes. Turn the right way out. Put the shoes on the doll and secure with a couple of stitches.

INDEX

A
abbreviations 7

B
Baby Bear 60–1
Beast, the 74–7
Beauty 72–4
Beauty & the Beast 68–71

C
casting off 9
casting on 8
chain stitch 13
crochet hook 6
crocheting a chain 11

D
Dame Gothel 32–4
decreasing
   k2tog 10
   p2tog 10
   s1, k2tog, psso 10
   ssk 10

E
embroidery needle 6
equipment 6
extended garter stitch 11

F
Father Bear 56–7
filling 7
French knot 13

G
Goldilocks 54–5
Goldilocks & the Three Bears 50–3
Grandmother, the 21–3
Gretel 45–6

H
Hansel 42–4
Hansel & Gretel 38–41
hiding & weaving in ends 13

I
increasing
   inc1 10
   m1 10

J
joining pieces 12

K
knit stitch 8
knitting needles 6

L
lace stitch 11
Little Red Riding Hood 14–17
   knitting 18–20

M
mattress stitch 12
Mother Bear 58–9

O
oversewing 12

P
picking up stitches along an edge 12
polyester toy filling 7
purl stitch 9

R
Rapunzel 26–9
   knitting 30–1
Rapunzel's Prince 35–7
reshaping 11

S
safety pins 6
satin stitch 13
scissors 6
sewing needle 6
sewing thread 7
Sisters, the 78–9
stitch holder 6
stitches
   casting off 9
   casting on 8
   chain 13
   decreasing k2tog 10
   decreasing p2tog 10
   decreasing s1, k2tog, psso 10
   decreasing ssk 10
   extended garter stitch 11
   French knot 13
   increasing inc1 10
   increasing m1 10
   knit stitch 8
   lace stitch 11
   purl stitch 9
   satin 13
   stocking 9
   straight 13
straight stitch 13

T
tape measure 6
tapestry needle 6
tension 7
Three Little Pigs, the 62–5
   knitting 66–7

W
water-soluble pen 7
Wicked Witch, the 47
Wolf, the 24–5

Y
yarn 7
yarn needle 6